Amazing Sounds in a Midwestern Town

Columbus, Indiana: Small City with a Big Musical Heritage

BYRON CARTWRIGHT

PathBinder
Publishing LLC
COLUMBUS, INDIANA

Published by PathBinder Publishing
P.O. Box 2611
Columbus, IN 47202
www.PathBinderPublishing.com

Edited by Doug Showalter
Covers designed by Paul J. Hoffman
Cover photo of the Columbus City Band, 1912,
by the Bartholomew County Historical Society

First published in 2025
Manufactured in the United States

ISBN: 978-1-955088-87-9
Library of Congress Control Number: 2025903416

NO AI TRAINING ALLOWED

To the memory of E. Wayne Berry,
who influenced many as a music professor and choral conductor,
but had the most profound impact through his service playing and
accompanying congregational singing as an organist.

Preface

Amazing Sounds in a Midwestern Town is not a title to catch your eye or imagination when selecting a book to read. When one discovers Columbus, Indiana, is the town referenced, some might realize the exceptional architectural significance of this city (population c. 50,000 in 2020). But, to connect the adjective "amazing" to the town's musical development since its earliest days, seems overstated, at best—ridiculous, at worst. However, I maintain the claim of my title and am committed to the distinction of this small city and its quite noteworthy musical achievements and personalities during a period of 120 years, from 1846-1966–the timeframe of my account. Columbus residents have a rich musical history to know, value, and share. The Columbus music story can be engaging for lovers of music and history. It can also provide positive motivation for possibilities of other mid-size communities. Music does not belong solely to the metropolis.

To whet your interest and possibly your choice for reading, I list some reasons for my audacious claims—these facts and more are detailed in the following pages. The Four Freshmen, who had musical ties to the Barbour family in Columbus in the late 1940s, went on to influence pop groups such as the Beach Boys, the Lettermen, and Manhattan Transfer. In music education, Columbus had a famous and influential conservatory of music housed in an exceptional facility more than forty years *before* Indiana University's powerhouse school of music was established.

In classical music, the state's oldest symphony orchestra was not founded in the capital city of Indianapolis, as one might expect, but in Columbus, and more than a decade before the Indianapolis Symphony. The national organization of public school music educators, or MTNA as it is known today, held some of its earliest organizational meetings in Columbus, at the conservatory mentioned above, due to the efforts of two men you have probably never heard of—Benjamin Hutchins and Artemas Nixon Johnson.

The Irwin-Sweeney-Miller family—so often studied in relationship to business, philanthropy, and architecture—was equally tied to exceptional musical progress, people, and programs throughout the entire span of this book. The founder of the family's fortune set the pace. Joseph Ireland Irwin led music at his church for almost twenty-six years, while he progressed quickly from poor shopkeeper to banker, to entrepreneur, to wealthiest man in the state at his death in 1910. His thriving business successes did not overpower or detract from his volunteer investment in music for more than a quarter of a century, and his descendants continued his example to help make music happen for many people. They did not just use the family fortune to make more money for themselves.

Irwin-Sweeney-Miller women were particularly remarkable in music leadership at church and throughout the musical world, exercising their influence powerfully in the community, state, and beyond. Finally, the person who benefitted the most from Irwin-Sweeney-Miller musical investment was E. Wayne Berry. Though only a few may have heard of him, his forty years in worship ministry at First Christian Church of Columbus, and his musical educational legacy through teaching at Butler University, Franklin College, and the Cincinnati Bible Seminary spread music to thousands of people. He taught hundreds of students piano, organ, music theory, composition, and music ministry, and his students went on to teach others, thus, his legacy continues to this day. He was the musical mentor for both my wife and me.

Threads woven into the following chapters include family, faith, wealth, and influence, recalling men and women who claimed a somewhat unlikely Hoosier locale as home. These influencers—their stories and their music—figured prominently throughout the 120-year span of this book. This modest-sized, but very distinctive Midwestern town has its own voice to share—from pioneer days, through wars, recessions, the gilded age, automotive inventions, industrial achievement, and musical delight, one can find compelling history in America's heartland.

Table of Contents

Section V: Insights

Section VI: Finale

What to Expect

As you read, think of this book as a large musical work.

Chapter One: Overture introduces you to the author's occasion for writing, what's coming, and provides clues for what and why.

Chapter Two: The Stage is Set before Columbus provides the greater historical setting for the story.

Chapters Three through Nine: The story unfolds in chronological order (more or less). Characters are introduced, dates are given, historical context is provided for the 120-year time frame. Occasionally, the author provides some special information to help with understanding and connecting the dots.

Chapters Ten through Thirteen: Author's imagined first-person cameo appearances of four key characters: Joseph I. Irwin, W. G. Irwin, Elsie Sweeney, and E. Wayne Berry. These "get-better-acquainted" chapters can be read apart from the unfolding story.

Chapters Fourteen through Seventeen: Insights present detailed information about four subjects related to the story. These are "behind-the-scenes" studies.

Chapter Eighteen Finale: This wraps it all up with a "beautiful bow and a humble bow."

Notes:

- There are many references to Irwin-Sweeney-Miller Family members. The Musical Family Tree at the end of Chapter ten will help keep them straight.
- Will Irwin was always known as W. G. or "Unk" by his nieces and nephews.
- Hugh Thomas Miller's name always appeared as "Hugh Th."
- The Cincinnati Bible Seminary is abbreviated CBS.
- The Christian Chapel, Tabernacle Church of Christ, and First Christian Church were names of the same congregation over time.
- Without trying to be too redundant, the author has repeated the historical context of important people and events for better comprehension.

—Byron Cartwright

SECTION I:

OVERTURE

Chapter One: It All Came Together

I have found it strange that a Midwestern boy like me ended up in the Deep South—nineteen years in metropolitan Atlanta, and, more recently, twelve years in eastern Alabama. My world started out very much defined by Indiana and Ohio, with a little Illinois and Kentucky thrown in. It was a comfortable, Midwestern mix.

However, *my* story—as musician, author, and lover of history—is woven into this book. Although I have strong ties to Indianapolis and Cincinnati, Columbus provided seeds of interest sown in childhood, nurtured by high school milestones, and rooted firmly in college-study connections. Advanced research at Southern Seminary, Louisville, Kentucky, brought my interest in Columbus' music history to full flower. Delightful research pilgrimages to Columbus, beginning in the early 1980s, coupled with invaluable assistance from Margaret Dismore, soprano/archivist extraordinaire, culminated in a two-volume dissertation for my Doctor of Musical Arts degree which I received in 1989.

Some information contained in the following chapters is drawn from my dissertation and includes earlier historical research, conversations, and letters from my musical mentor, Professor E. Wayne Berry. Copies of the dissertation are in the Bartholomew County Historical Society's holdings and in the library of First Christian Church in Columbus.

More recent investigation and personal experience combined powerfully during a visit to Columbus after my wife and I retired, and after the worst part of the pandemic was over in the summer of 2021. Upon returning to Columbus for the first time in thirty-two years, threads from my lifetime and 50-year musical career meshed into the story of *Amazing Sounds in a Midwestern Town: Columbus, Indiana: Small City with a Big Musical Heritage* I now share.

It all came together in Columbus, and here is how I fit into the story.

I was born in Indianapolis, Indiana, in 1949, and I lived in Indianapolis and Cincinnati, Ohio, twice by the time I was in college. During my second Indianapolis sojourn my family lived in Broad Ripple, close to Butler University, where Clowes Memorial Hall is located. During my second Cincinnati sojourn, I attended Cincinnati Bible Seminary (later renamed Cincinnati Christian University, which closed in 2019).

Growing up, I heard of the prominent Irwin-Sweeney-Miller family—their business acumen and accomplishments in ministry, architecture, and education—but never associated their philanthropy with my world. Although the Irwin-Sweeney-Miller family and my family were not related, both families were closely associated with Christian Churches of the Restoration Movement. My parents had taken me to visit First Christian Church in Columbus more than once. During childhood, I aspired to become an architect, therefore I was fascinated by the church's distinctive modern architecture. My interest in its outstanding music program came later when I pursued music as my college major.

Education was Key

During musical studies at Cincinnati Bible Seminary, my music theory professor, piano/organ professor, and first college choir director was E. Wayne Berry. I studied with Professor Berry throughout undergraduate and graduate degrees at the seminary. Berry grew up in Columbus, and shared fascinating stories about music at First Christian Church, where he had served as organist from 1925-1966 (the longest tenure of any paid staff in the congregation's history). Berry resigned in 1966, and with his wife, Frances, moved to Cincinnati to expand the music department at Cincinnati Bible Seminary, where he had taught part-time since 1953. During my first Cincinnati sojourn—elementary and middle school years—my parents took me to Berry's musical programs presented at the college's chapel. My mother loved his choral and organ music. I became a student of Professor Berry during my second Cincinnati sojourn, when I enrolled as a freshman at Cincinnati Bible Seminary for the fall semester 1967, following graduation from Broad Ripple High School in Indianapolis the preceding spring.

Broad Ripple's high school graduation was held at Butler University Field House, and I had attended many concerts, symphonies, music competitions, and my first two operas at Clowes Memorial Hall on Butler's campus. Nearby was the Hilton U. Brown Theater, where Broadway musicals (often featuring original cast members) were presented as part of their regular "Starlight Musicals" series every summer. I had no realization of Irwin-Sweeney-Miller connections to my high school musical experiences at Butler University, Clowes Hall, Indianapolis Symphony, or Metropolitan opera performances at Clowes.

Over time, I learned the Irwins, Sweeneys, and Millers had been generous benefactors to Butler ever since 1850, when Benjamin Irwin served on a committee with abolitionist Ovid Butler to establish Northwestern Christian University—later renamed Butler University. A century later, Benjamin Irwin's descendent Elsie Sweeney's interest and philanthropy helped make Clowes Memorial Hall a reality. She, E. Wayne Berry, and First Christian's choir spear-headed significant fund-raising for the Indianapolis Symphony Orchestra as far back as 1941, when the orchestra was only eleven years old.

Symphony concerts at Clowes were conducted by Izler Solomon, father of David Solomon, who graduated with me at Broad Ripple. Izler Solomon was a driving force in the development of the Indianapolis Symphony, and he, together with Elsie Sweeney, successfully advocated building Clowes Hall on the Butler campus. Thus, Izler Solomon and Elsie Sweeney's combined efforts laid a foundation which impacted and expanded my high school musical world—a foundation which I always valued—but one which included more connections I did not realize for many years.

The Irwin-Sweeney-Miller family invested richly in the education and career of E. Wayne Berry from the 1920s on. Elsie Sweeney and her sister, Nettie Sweeney Miller, were his prime benefactors and chief influencers. The sisters' wealth and prestige opened doors for him, and their generous financial investments yielded incredible benefits for Berry, personally and professionally. Nettie Sweeney Miller's children, Clementine Miller Tangeman and J. Irwin Miller, also participated with Berry in his exceptional musical endeavors for First Christian Church, the Columbus community, and the entire state of Indiana.

It Finally Starts to Come Together

In the early 1980s, during doctoral work at Southern Baptist Theological Seminary in Louisville, I began focusing on my dissertation. It was to be entitled "A History of the Music Ministry of First Christian Church, Columbus, Indiana." Information provided by Professor Berry fueled my initial motivation. However, the longer I researched, the more I discovered an underlying, equally rich Columbus musical heritage, stretching back to the community's very early days.

My study revealed many musicians and developments, as far back as Joseph I. Irwin in 1846. Early Columbus musical history was closely tied to his family; the Irwin family expanded to include Sweeneys, and eventually Millers in the generations which followed. This family's musical influence was significant beginning in 1846, during years of the Christian Chapel of 1852, and Tabernacle Church of Christ of 1879–both earlier names of today's First Christian Church, constructed in 1942.

Twists, Turns and Roadblocks

Although most people publish their doctoral dissertations, I did not—life happened. During the last six months of 1989 I changed careers; my family moved from greater Cincinnati to Phoenix, Arizona; and my wife gave up her successful piano studio. I began a demanding music position in a large church, completed my dissertation and doctorate, sold a house, bought and redecorated a house, made repeated flights between Cincinnati and Phoenix to tie up all manner of loose ends, and graduated from Southern Seminary. It was an overwhelming and exhausting time. Life's interruptions and demands forced me to put my dissertation on a shelf—gladly out of mind when completed—where it remained for decades. I had wanted to publish findings which became so compelling for me, however more immediate, pressing challenges of family survival took priority in my life for years to come.

Pandemic Refocus

Now, I skip ahead more than thirty years, after the Covid pandemic changed so much of life. At the conclusion of spring semester, 2021, Katie and I retired as music professors from Point University, West Point, Georgia, (a complicated and completely different story, in and of itself—details of which are published in my memoirs, *Connections and Reflections* available through Amazon). We had served on the faculty there for twenty-eight years.

As the pandemic waned, in July 2021 we ventured forth into the real world again. I'm not sure whether it was a whim or intentional trip, but it was our first return to Columbus, Indiana, since 1989–thirty-two years earlier. Our lives in the meantime had been fulfilling, but also crisscrossed with detours—some good, some difficult—life happens. In Columbus, the two of us retraced my dissertation memories. I was able to relive with Katie many connections she had not been able to share because of her career and rearing our two children. We spent two nights at The Inn at Irwin Gardens (formerly the Irwin-Sweeney-Miller mansion for over a century).

It was an "Ah-Ha!" visit for me. I realized just how much interesting musical history had not been shared, and that history was mine to share. Plus, I now had the Internet at my disposal, as well as other research not available thirty-two years ago. I also determined that even though my dissertation included exceptional musical progress through the 1980s, a more realistic scope for publication would be Columbus' early musical story beginning in 1846 and culminating in 1966, when E. Wayne Berry resigned from

Author's Note: *In this photo, Katie Bennett Cartwright is seated at the piano in the Irwin-Sweeney-Miller mansion, July 2021. Though not the original instrument, the piano is in the music room where Elsie Sweeney's Steinway grand was located. Miss Elsie, as she was known, practiced and performed here; she hosted E. Wayne Berry for rehearsals and performances; and it was Miss Elsie who made connections at Juilliard for Berry's graduate study in piano. Miss Elsie's niece and nephew, Clementine Miller Tangeman and J. Irwin Miller, created music here together with Wayne Berry from the 1920s through 1950s. Katie and I ate a delicious breakfast in this special room now part of the Inn at Irwin Gardens. It was nostalgic for us to create a memory in a place where the man who brought us together made music! Photo by Byron Cartwright*

First Christian Church to develop the Cincinnati Bible Seminary music department full-time. My scope for this book was defined; my vision began to materialize.

What is Different About This Book

Many people have researched Columbus, Indiana. Much of what they have written has concentrated on architecture, business, and the general philanthropy of the Irwin-Sweeney-Miller family. Musical life of the town, especially in its earliest years, and the musical impact of the Irwins, Sweeneys, and Millers combined with E. Wayne Berry has not been detailed. There have been many others whose musical contributions have been significant: Amasa Cobb, Benjamin Hutchins, Artemas Nixon Johnson, William and Jennie Bates, Arthur Mason, Will Harding, G. Chester and Elise Kitzinger, Claude Smith, Ida Edinburn, Gary Davis, the Crump family, George Schwartzkopf, Edwin and Hazel Crouch.

Early musical history uncovered through my research and personal information from Professor Berry (his college classes, conversations and personal letters) provided a treasure-trove of information just as interesting as the musical impact of the town's leading family. Except for trust funds established for long-term maintenance, Irwin-Sweeney-Miller influence at First Christian Church essentially ceased by 1966. Therefore, I present the story which has fascinated me most: the days of an amazing musical Midwestern town, 1846 through 1966.

Wait! The Backstory is not Complete!

However, there is more to the backstory of this book. E. Wayne Berry hired Katie Bennett upon completion of her master's degree from Eastern Illinois University. She became full-time piano and music theory instructor at Cincinnati Bible Seminary in 1971. Berry hired me the same year as a graduate assistant, and that is when Katie and I met. After earning a master's degree under Berry as my major professor, I was hired as a full-time choral director and voice teacher in 1972. Thus, Katie and I met and began our teaching careers together because E. Wayne Berry hired both of us.

Katie Bennett became Katie Bennett Cartwright on March 8, 1974, and Professor Berry was organist for our wedding. A few years later, I took over leadership of the concert choir which Berry had conducted, and I was named chairman of Cincinnati Bible Seminary's music department—the same position Professor Berry held until his retirement in 1974. Strangely enough, I had hoped, strategized, and worked to achieve these goals since age fifteen—how audacious. But truth is stranger than fiction and these goals became reality by age thirty.

I had followed E. Wayne Berry's footsteps in many ways, and he had provided the inspiration for my doctoral dissertation. From early 1980s through 1989 I became thoroughly engrossed in Columbus, Indiana, its music, and Berry's forty-year association with First Christian Church. My research became a wonderful escape from complicated reality, and gradually I began to identify and comprehend the impact of connections I now present in this book.

Realities Revealed

During my second Indianapolis sojourn (high school) I benefited from Irwin-Sweeney-Miller investments in Butler University, Clowes Memorial Hall, and the Indianapolis Symphony before ever studying with Professor Berry. I was totally ignorant of the prominent family's musical investments in Berry's world, too, or their investments which enriched my world. Furthermore, the Irwin-Sweeney-Miller musical investment in E. Wayne Berry was also transmitted through him into the teaching careers of my wife and me—an investment we will cherish for the rest of our lives—an investment we endeavor to honor.

Both Katie and I completed fifty-year careers as music professionals in education and ministry. We served together on two college faculties and with congregations in five states. Both of us received a rich legacy because of E. Wayne Berry, First Christian Church, the Irwin-Sweeney-Miller family, and all that unfolded in the musical life of Columbus, Indiana, an amazing Midwestern town.

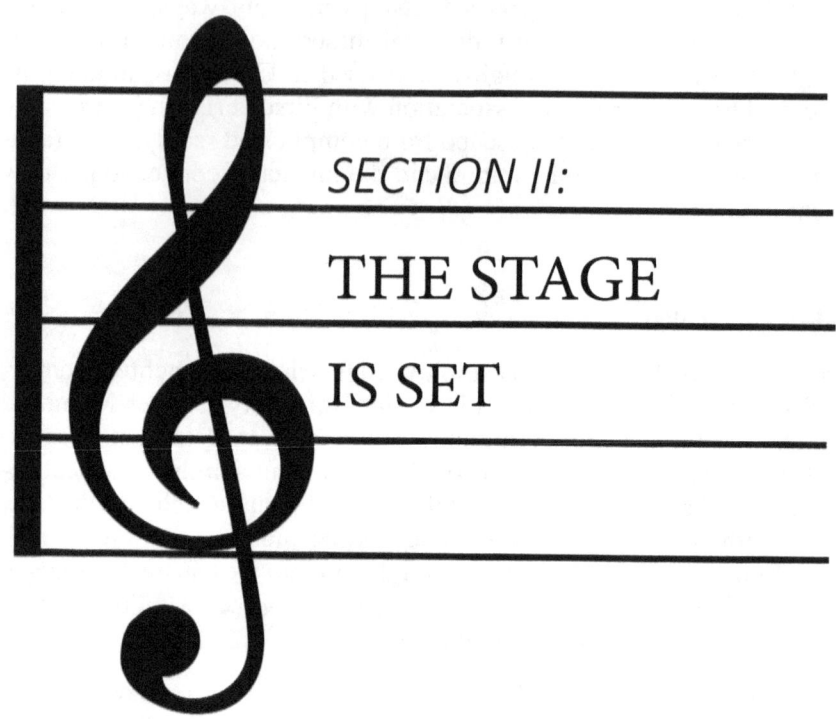

SECTION II:

THE STAGE
IS SET

Chapter Two: Before Columbus

We might think nineteenth-century Indiana history is the only context for music which developed in the amazing Midwestern town of Columbus, Indiana. However, the bigger picture of world history paints a fascinating backdrop which deserves a brief overview.

In the Treaty of Paris, 1763, France relinquished control of vast lands in North America to England. The British gained territory west of its Atlantic coast colonies—all the way to the Mississippi River. For a time, the king of England forbade English colonists from settling west of the Appalachian Mountains. (Obviously, his prohibition did not last long.) French, Native Americans, English, and early settlers all claimed the land for settlement. Sometimes they agreed, but more often they fought; blood was shed, and great numbers perished. Native Americans died in large numbers, not only in battle, but because they had no immunity against diseases Europeans and others brought. Our history included great tragedy.

George Rogers Clark explored the huge territory and claimed much of it for the esteemed Colony of Virginia while Patrick Henry was governor. Soon Virginia and the Congress of the Confederation squabbled for control of the territory. But it took another Treaty of Paris, September 3, 1783, to end the American Revolution for the newly formed United States of America to gain practically limitless territory for future expansion. The landmark 1783 Treaty of Paris—one of the most consequential for modern history—not only recognized the existence of the United States as an independent nation, but also ceded a vast amount of land east of the Mississippi to the new nation. A portion of the ceded area was known as the Old Northwest, and was larger than the original thirteen colonies combined. Today we know much of the Old Northwest as our American Midwest, and it includes Ohio, Indiana, Illinois, Michigan, Wisconsin, and part of Minnesota.

Benjamin Franklin, John Jay, and John Adams were extremely skilled negotiators for the United States in meetings which hashed-out terms for the 1783 Treaty of Paris; they returned home with huge concessions from the British. The fledgling United States was now larger than many powerful European empires.

In 1787, the US Congress passed the Northwest Ordinance, which outlined important provisions for future statehood. The provisions secured religious freedom, provided for public education, and guaranteed no slavery in the territory. Although exact figures are difficult to determine, at the time of the American Revolution, the slave population may have approached twenty percent. Mind-boggling dreams and possibilities took shape as the United States grew westward. Settlers came from European nations, and huge numbers relocated from other places in the United States to chart their future.

Although President George Washington wanted Native Americans to be treated justly, his lofty goal was not achieved as droves of settlers poured into the vast territory, claiming their stake on what had been Native lands. The situation was overwhelming for the developing nation; frontier behavior often did not match lofty vision—or negotiated agreements. Settlers and Native Americans engaged in bloody confrontations. Tribes such as Delaware, Miami, Shawnee, and Illinois suffered and were eventually defeated and/or relocated by the government. Names associated with the territory, such as Tecumseh, Potawatomi, "Mad Anthony Wayne," Captain Zachary Taylor, and William Henry Harrison, became famous—or infamous—in American history.

The land of the Northwest Territory was rich in natural resources, highly prized, and worth fighting over. What some called "civilization" occurred at a remarkable pace during the end of the eighteenth and early nineteenth centuries. Lasting peace did not really prevail until the early nineteenth century. Everything happened so quickly.

On December 11, 1816, President James Madison signed the congressional resolution to admit Indiana as the nineteenth state of the union. The state name harkened back to inhabitants who had preceded white men and women. Indiana's first capital was Vincennes, then Corydon, before Indianapolis became the state capital in 1823. General John Tipton had purchased land on which the small settlement Tiptona was established in 1820, but the town's name was changed to Columbus in 1821. Later the same year, the state legislature established Bartholomew County, naming it in honor of a famous Hoosier militiaman, General Joseph Bartholomew. The town of Columbus, the state of Indiana, and the Midwestern United States grew at incredible pace. By 1900 Bartholomew County was identified as the mean center of population in the United States. Cultural growth quickly followed numerical growth.

SECTION III

THE STORY
UNFOLDS

Chapter Three: Progress Comes Quickly

In settlements throughout the sprawling nation, pioneer families first had to focus on clearing the wilderness, building homes, growing food, and reorganizing their lives in a new, sometimes hostile land. Axes, plows, shovels, and hammers were the main tools people used as they worked together, and weapons were always close by for protection. Settlers sought meaningful ways to form tight-knit communities. Communication and cooperation were keys to every aspect of everyday life; people worked together, helped each other and spent precious free time enjoying each other; formal social and musical organizations were yet to emerge. Churches were very important to frontier life, not only for religious reasons, but for social interaction, too. Worship, education, and community events led to distinctive cultural identities combining prevailing English, Irish, Scottish, and German influences from prior homes and homelands.

Such was the situation in Bartholomew County, Indiana. However, nineteenth-century pioneers soon laid foundations for many significant developments which rapidly unfolded and intersected in the early decades of Indiana statehood. The pioneers' vision and resourcefulness cannot be underestimated, and it is summarized below.

Congregations Impacted Communities

Various religious faiths were represented among the settlers of Bartholomew County. Presbyterians, Methodists, and Baptists were among the largest denominations represented, but there were also Lutherans, Moravians, Friends, Shakers, Anglicans, and Catholics; African-American congregations were separate from others. People with similar beliefs began meeting together in log cabins belonging to their friends. They used music they already knew or brought with them from eastern areas of the country and lands of the "old world" across the ocean. There were few instruments of any sort—perhaps a fiddle, banjo, or in rare cases, a reed pump organ. Printed music was essentially non-existent, and only the privileged owned small, personal pocket psalters or hymnals.

One of the first religious groups to organize (on April 26, 1823,) called themselves the Columbus Baptized Church. In October 1824, they changed their name to Hope Baptist Church of Christ.[1] The congregation erected its own house of worship; and one member, Benjamin Irwin, gave a corner of his farm, where a log church thirty feet square was built.[2] The church's first minister was Joseph Fassett, who was ordained in May 1824.[3] Fassett preached in all the Baptist churches of the county and was also very influential as a teacher. Benjamin Irwin was one of Fassett's students and was regarded as a capable minister in his own right. He often preached for the Hope congregation and performed many marriage ceremonies.

Benjamin Irwin became a member of the state legislature from Bartholomew County, and in 1850 he served on a committee with lawyer and abolitionist Ovid Butler to organize Northwestern Christian University (renamed Butler University in 1877).[4] It is important to remember that Bartholomew County was part of the Northwest Territory, and slavery had been outlawed, but it was still a hotly debated subject. The new Christian university took a firm stand paving the way in higher education and promoting ideals of freedom and equality during the decade when national debate finally exploded into civil war.

Benjamin Irwin and his descendants continued to voice their strong beliefs through generations to come. The Irwin family grew to include Sweeneys within a few decades, and later, Millers. The family strongly rejected slavery, demonstrated Christian faith, and maintained generous support for education, especially Butler University, continuing through the twentieth century. Irwin-Sweeney-Miller influence became closely woven into the musical story of Columbus, too.

Brief Summary of Restoration Movement History

From 1823 to 1830 Alexander Campbell (1788-1866) published the *Christian Baptist* and sent it to fellow Baptist ministers throughout Bartholomew County.[5] Joseph Fassett soon found himself in sympathy with the beliefs of Alexander Campbell and began to preach Campbell's ideas in his sermons. The White Water Baptist Association took opposition to Campbell's beliefs as expressed in Fassett's preaching, but the Hope congregation continued to pursue its own course and withdrew from the White Water Baptist Association in October 1829.[6]

The Baptist name was rejected, and the congregation decided to call itself the Church of God in Christ in New Hope.[7] The New Hope community where the church was located was a few miles northeast of Columbus, and was a small but vibrant town, dominated by farming and related needs.

At this point there was no Baptist church in Columbus, nor any other congregation following the ideas of Alexander Campbell. Congregations which aligned themselves with the views of Alexander Campbell and other preachers—Thomas Campbell, Barton W. Stone, Walter Scott, and John Smith—became part of the Restoration Movement[8] (also known as the Stone-Campbell Movement). Two basic goals of this distinctly American movement were the authority of scripture and the unity of all believers. The Restoration Movement grew rapidly in nineteenth-century America.

Within a few years, some members of the New Hope congregation moved to Columbus, and other residents of Columbus became part of the New Hope church. By 1839 the congregation numbered 175. About this time a frame building was built (again on the corner of Benjamin Irwin's farm) to replace the original log cabin church.[9]

In 1841 a frame building was erected in Columbus to accommodate church services which then alternated between New Hope and Columbus.[10] This building was destroyed by fire, and in 1852 a brick building known as the Christian Chapel was built in Columbus to replace it. Services continued to alternate between the Christian Chapel in Columbus and the New Hope congregation until 1855. On July 22, 1855, the Christian Church of Columbus was organized as a separate congregation with about sixty members.[11]

Early Musical Influences

The first mention of music leadership for the church occurs before the separation of the New Hope and Columbus congregations. A twenty-one-year-old Joseph I. Irwin (nephew of Benjamin Irwin) came to Columbus in 1846 to accept a position as salesman in a dry goods store. He took an active part in the congregation from that time, and one of the tasks he performed was leading the singing.[12] Music was important to Irwin, and he continued to lead singing for twenty-six years, while also becoming a successful businessman, community, state, and church leader.

Even as he achieved social and business status, he found time for music in his busy life. After he stopped leading singing at church, he continued to lend substantial leadership and financial support to the church's music program throughout his life. Irwin's impact on every aspect of life in Columbus was profound; his musical example and influence became powerful—in family, church, and community matters.

Perhaps the most important external influence on the music of the congregation, and, indeed, the entire community at this time, was the singing

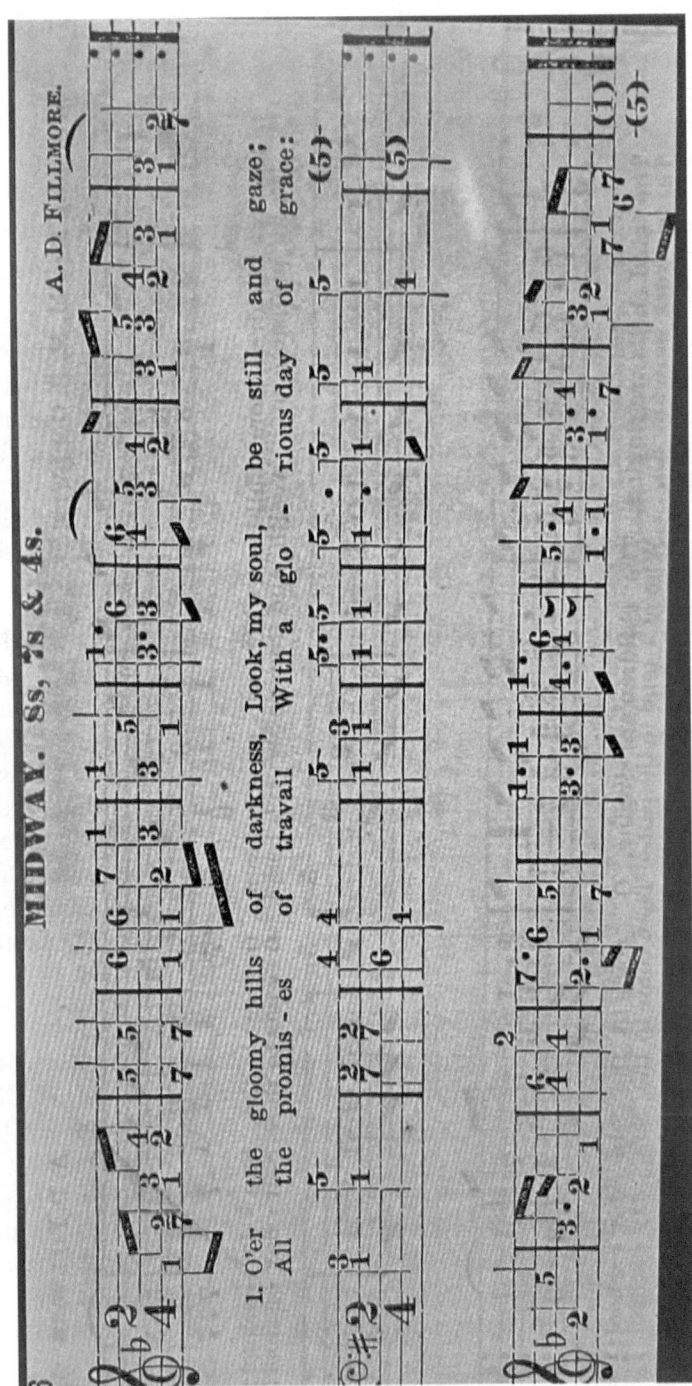

A. D. Fillmore's musical notation for William Williams'
hymn, "O'er the Gloomy Hills of Darkness."

school movement. Singing schools were popular throughout the nation as favorite sources of recreation, social interaction, and musical improvement. They had started in the northeastern United States in the mid-to-late eighteenth century and spread quickly throughout the growing nation as a means of improving congregational singing. Singing schools were usually conducted in churches. Early in the spring of 1855 (the same year that New Hope and Columbus congregations formally and peacefully separated), A. D. Fillmore of Cincinnati, Ohio, taught a singing school at New Hope church.[13]

Fillmore (1823-1870) was a well-known music teacher and singer whose reputation was further enhanced by the various books he compiled for use in singing schools he conducted. Besides containing many hymns, Fillmore's books included lessons on general musicianship, and set forth his own system of musical notation involving numerals on the lines and spaces of the staff. In the classes taught at New Hope, Fillmore used his book, *The Western Minstrel*. Each class member paid one dollar for tuition and fifty cents for a book.[14]

Joseph I. Irwin and A. D. Fillmore shared similar backgrounds, which influenced the future of music in Columbus. Fillmore was just a year older than Irwin, and he, too, had a fine voice. Both succeeded in business and were part of the Restoration Movement of churches, yet neither followed Alexander Campbell's teaching to the letter—at least not as far as music was concerned. Campbell advocated a cappella singing without the use of printed music; he felt musical notation and printed words distracted from the spiritual aspect of congregational singing. However, Fillmore used his own musical notation in singing schools and in his first printed hymnal, *The Christian Psalmist 1847*, which was printed especially for Restoration Movement congregations.

His notation is likely what Joseph I. Irwin learned in Fillmore's 1855 singing school at New Hope and continued to use at the Christian Chapel in Columbus (which changed its name to Tabernacle Church of Christ in 1879). Furthermore, Irwin had been leading singing in the new Christian Chapel of 1852, which had a pipe organ. Unlike Alexander Campbell, he had no problem with instrumental music or printed music notation. He maintained a life-long connection with Fillmore Brothers Publishing, the company A. D.'s three sons established in 1874 in Cincinnati. Irwin's last personal hymnal, *The Praise Hymnal* 1896, was published by Fillmore Brothers and used by Tabernacle Church of Christ congregation. Irwin used his song-leading skills for over a quarter of a century.

It is reasonable to assume Joseph I. Irwin and A. D. Fillmore became friends through music and the Restoration Movement. Fillmore's singing school laid a foundation for Joseph Irwin's musical philosophy beyond singing and song leading. Irwin and his descendants were lovers and generous supporters of music, and were key figures in amazing music developments at church and in the community.

Joseph I. Irwin (August 6, 1824-August 10, 1910)

Although Joseph I. Irwin's life and business accomplishments have been chronicled and celebrated by many authors, the highlights below serve as review of his achievements and give context for his musical contributions, which have not been specifically recognized heretofore. Joseph Ireland Irwin was born on August 6, 1824, on a farm four miles north of Columbus.[15] Although his family left Bartholomew County for a time, Irwin returned to Columbus (age twenty-one) in the spring of 1846 to work as a clerk in the Alden and Snyder store at Fourth and Washington streets. Irwin's father (another charter member at New Hope Church and brother to Benjamin Irwin) had died when Joseph was twelve, leaving him responsible for the farm, his mother, and three sisters. Joseph Irwin felt he could make more money in town, but promised his mother he would remain on the farm until he was twenty-one. When he arrived in Columbus he had only 30 cents and a formal education that had concluded at age fifteen.[16] Nevertheless, Irwin was incredibly successful in all of his ventures. He saved his money and purchased thirty acres of land, divided it and sold portions which became the heart of Columbus. Successful real estate dealings also helped him raise money to finance his own dry goods store in 1850.[17]

A hymnal belonging to Joseph I. Irwin. // Byron Cartwright

He launched many more successful businesses throughout his life to benefit Columbus.

Author's note: *In 1974 upon his retirement, Professor E. Wayne Berry gave me a stack of music and hymnals, all of which were put in boxes* *and stacked away. Decades later, I discovered this hymnal, which had belonged to Joseph I. Irwin and was engraved with his name on the cover. I was surprised and delighted to have this book which had belonged to such a distinguished man. Irwin died in 1910, and this was probably his last hymnal. It was copyrighted in 1896 by the Fillmore Brothers in Cincinnati, Ohio, a music publishing company founded by A. D. Fillmore's sons. Fillmore had conducted the singing school (which enriched Irwin's song-leading), and his sons, J. H., Fred A., and Charles M., established a music publishing company which printed music for congregational singing in large numbers of churches throughout the nation, including Columbus. The Fillmore and Irwin families helped pave the way of sharing music for generations to come. What a happy discovery for my library.*

Joseph Irwin was a man of integrity, highly respected as a businessman and Christian leader; he married Harriet Clementine Glanton in 1850. People began to trust him to the point they left money in his store for safekeeping. In 1871, Columbus was shaken by the failure of McEwen and Sons Bank; losses totaled about half a million dollars. It is likely this failure, plus the confidence Bartholomew County residents already had in Irwin's ability to keep their money safe, caused Joseph Irwin to establish his own bank in 1871 under the private banking law of Indiana.[18] The bank continued very successfully in the family's hands as a private business until 1928, when Irwin's Bank merged with the Union Trust Company.

Irwin also started Bartholomew County's system of turnpike roads in 1866 and at one time owned nearly all of the toll-roads in the county.[19] To maintain communication between his Columbus store and a toll-gate on the road west of town, he installed the first telephone line in Indiana in 1878.[20] Other business ventures included organizing the National Tinplate Company; erection of the Indianapolis, Columbus, and Southern Traction Line; and establishment of Union Starch and Refining Company. He was industrious and innovative, yet not too busy with business to lead singing at church.

Irwin actively supported the work of Christian higher education. In 1868 he was elected as a director of Northwestern Christian University, and in 1871 he served as president of the board.[21] Throughout his life he provided generous financial support to the university. Another Restoration Movement school, Johnson Bible College (now Johnson University) in Kimberlin Heights, Tennessee, received a substantial gift from Joseph Irwin to help rebuild after fire destroyed the college's main building.[22]

Besides business and educational interests, Irwin was active in Republican politics in Indiana. Between 1862 and 1876 he was county chairman, and he served as a delegate to the Republican National Convention in 1872 and 1874.[23] He was well-acquainted with President Abraham Lincoln, and among his close personal friends were Presidents James A. Garfield and Benjamin Harrison. When Harrison became president, he offered Irwin the cabinet post of treasurer of the United States, which he declined.[24]

The Christian Church in Columbus benefited from Irwin's leadership in other areas besides music. He served the congregation faithfully for many years as Sunday school superintendent and elder. If the church ran behind with the minister's salary or other expenses, he paid them; and by 1871 he was contributing twenty percent of the congregation's yearly income. When the Christian churches of the county organized the Bartholomew County Christian Missionary Association in 1887, Irwin served on the first board of officers.[25]

The varied talents and wealth of Joseph I. Irwin helped to establish many worthwhile causes in excellent fashion for the city of Columbus and the Christian Church. Irwin's role in maintaining quality music programs was significant until his death on August 13, 1910. Readers will note that Joseph I. Irwin's children (William G. and Linnie) continued his example, donating time and resources to many worthy projects.

Musical Development Comes Quickly

In 1872 two more individuals who possessed exceptional gifts came to Columbus, and to the Christian Church. Their talents, energy, and influence had a long-lasting effect on the church and the community's musical development. The first was Zachary Taylor Sweeney, who became the dynamic young preacher for the Christian Chapel. Z. T. Sweeney's involvement will be detailed later. The second person who became significantly involved with the congregation and particularly music in the community was Benjamin Miles Hutchins. Joseph I. Irwin, Z. T. Sweeney, and Benjamin Hutchins became close friends and a powerful force—often behind the scenes—for musical development. They shared vision, drive, and the ability to motivate others. People trusted and admired them.

Benjamin Miles Hutchins (December 29, 1838 - June 20, 1918)

Benjamin M. Hutchins was born in Morgan County, Ohio, as the fourth of nine children.[26] By the age of sixteen he had to make his own living (his father had died several years before), and he managed the family farm until 1859. After a brief stay in Iowa, he returned to Ohio in 1860 and formed a partnership with Harper Young in the oil business. In the spring of 1861 Hutchins came to Columbus, Indiana, but for only a few months. Following the outbreak of the Civil War he enlisted in the Union army in August 1861.[27] After being discharged in 1864, he returned to Ohio and resumed his oil business for two years, before transitioning to the music profession.

From 1866-1871 Hutchins was engaged in teaching music and conducting musical institutes throughout various parts of Indiana and other states. However, he returned to Columbus permanently in 1872 and started a music store in partnership with John B. Cobb, a former preach-

B. M. Hutchins //
Bartholomew County
Historical Society

er at the Christian Church and Joseph I. Irwin's brother-in-law. Noted for his fine baritone voice, Hutchins taught voice students after business was complete each day at the music store. Although he was self-educated as a musician, except for singing schools, Hutchins was regarded as a fine musician.

Hutchins transferred his membership to the Christian Chapel from the Baptist church on March 19, 1872.[28] It was not long before Joseph I. Irwin recognized Hutchins' musical gifts, especially his exceptional baritone voice, and turned the church's song leading over to him.[29] As mentioned earlier, Irwin had started leading singing at church when he was twenty-one, shortly after returning to Columbus in 1846. Irwin, now in his late forties, seized the moment to involve new leadership, and he enlisted Benjamin Hutchins, age thirty-four, to take over the music. Hutchins would exercise profound musical influence in the community for the rest of his life.

As a result of their common interests—music and the church—Hutchins and Irwin became lifelong friends. Together they provided wise leadership for the city and the congregation's musical development into the twentieth century. Hutchins' close relationship with the Cobb family was significant beyond his obvious business partnership at the music store. John B. Cobb was married to Joseph Irwin's sister, and they had two sons, John I. and Amasa (also known as Amp or A. B.), who also became key participants in music of the Christian Chapel. Amasa was the congregation's first named organist and directed the choir.[30] He was very involved in music of the community, too. Some years later John I. Cobb and Hutchins sang together in a quartet which was popular at church and in the community.

1872–Pivotal Year for Another Reason

The year 1872 was important in the life of the Christian Church, not only because Joseph I. Irwin, Z. T. Sweeney, Benjamin Hutchins, and John B. Cobb all established long-lasting relationships. It was also the year that the newspaper, *The Evening Republican*, was founded.[31] Newspaper articles regularly reported events at church and gave particular attention to musical programs at the Christian Chapel. *The Evening Republican* has provided more information about congregational life during the last twenty-eight years of the nineteenth century than any documents in the archives of First Christian Church.

Cultural life in Columbus was closely tied to church life, and church buildings were used for many functions besides worship. The Christian Chapel, built in 1852, was a large brick building for its time, seating approximately 450. Furthermore, it contained a pipe organ, not a reed organ (which would have been more typical for the day), and therefore provided an exceptional instrument for musical programs and accompaniments.[32] Although the Christian Chapel must have been a very fine venue for mid-nineteenth-century programs, it was not the outstanding facility that the congregation's 1879 or 1942 structures were to provide.

The Civil War may have slowed musical activity for a time, but it wasn't long afterward that musical life in the entire United States took on new energy. The East Coast's so-called "Gilded Age" included a musical impetus. It became common for music teachers to travel around the country, teaching lessons and training choirs in short-term classes known as normals. Benjamin Hutchins had been very successful teaching music in normals for several years following his Civil War military service. Normals became particularly popular in Columbus, and the newspaper recorded aspects of a normal in 1872 known as the Indiana Normal Academy of Music.[33] Music taught during normals was performed for public concerts.

At least two public concerts of the normal held during the summer of 1872 were presented at the Christian Chapel and reviewed in the newspaper.[34] *The Evening Republican* refers to a performance of "Inflammatus" from Rossini's *Stabat Mater*. Mrs. U. J. Hammond was the soprano soloist and was commended for her high Cs. This is the first reference to a performance of "Inflammatus," which remained a favorite of the Tabernacle congregation throughout the next century. Many decades later, Frances Pearce (who became Mrs. E. Wayne Berry) was often featured as soloist for the Rossini crowd-pleaser.

Author's note: Rossini's Stabat Mater had stirred European audiences since the 1840s, and the opera composer drew upon his dramatic style to set the ancient liturgical text. His thrilling soprano aria with chorus, "Inflammatus," was performed for an admiring Columbus audience in 1872. European tastes crossed the Atlantic to the American Midwest in about thirty years—amazingly fast in a time before recordings and mass communication. It is astonishing to note how music education had progressed since A. D. Fillmore's 1855 singing school and various musical normals held thereafter. The performance of this Stabat Mater movement indicates exceptional musical achievement which the Indiana Normal Academy of Music facilitated.

Normals and music conventions continued to be effective tools for music education in and around Columbus, and many of the classes and concerts were held at the Christian Chapel. A December 26, 1872, newspaper article reviewed a special Christmas Eve service at the church.[35] About 400 attended, and gifts were distributed to almost everyone present. A brass band played several pieces, and there was also singing by "a quartet of our best musicians."[36] This event was quite a Christmas party for a small community in 1872.

On May 6, 1873, the Christian Chapel featured a concert by the "best vocal talent in the city."[37] Admission was 25 cents. Tickets were sold at Cobb's music store or at the door by ladies of the church.

Benjamin Hutchins took a strong interest in all musical activities of Columbus. He was responsible to a large degree for spear-heading music education development in the entire town and was very eager to see music promoted in every aspect of community life. He wanted to make sure that others benefitted from the type of education he had been denied because of the Civil War. He wrote:

> *"Before enlisting in the army I had planned to go to school, but the excitement occasioned by the breaking out of war led me away from that purpose and after returning from the army, it seemed too late; therefore with thousands of other young men about my age who went into the army at the time they should have entered college, I have been crippled and handicapped, but I try to content myself because of the wonderful achievements of the Union army of which I was a part."[38]*

The Central Indiana Conservatory of Music

Hutchins' love of music and lack of formal education combined to provide the motivation for his efforts to establish a music school in Columbus. In 1874 he dissolved his partnership in the music store with John B. Cobb to encourage others to help him start such a school. He worked for two years, 1874-1876, to find the musical leadership he wanted. Eventually, Hutchins was able to convince William E. Bates and the Academy of Music in Madison, Indiana, to move to Columbus.[39] Furthermore, Hutchins persuaded Artemas Nixon Johnson from New York to lend his name and national reputation in establishing the Central Indiana Conservatory of Music in Columbus.[40] Establishment of this institution became extremely significant for the future musical progress of the town and the entire community.

Artemas Nixon Johnson (June 22, 1817–January 1, 1892)

Although A. N. Johnson's fame later declined, and he fell into oblivion for much of the early-to-mid-twentieth century, more recent scholarship reveals his fine musical credentials and impact on American musical life during the second half of the nineteenth century. Johnson was an organist and conductor who had studied with George Webb and Lowell Mason in Boston. He and esteemed musician Lowell Mason had worked closely together, but later he took issue with Mason's "Pestalozzian" system of vocal instruction and set forth his own "Johnson System" in opposition to Mason's. From 1842-1843 he studied music theory in Europe under the Swiss musician Frank Xaver Schnyder von Wartensee (1786-1868) at Frankfort am Main. Johnson compiled and published many books for musical instruction which have been re-discovered in recent years. During his lifetime, he had great musical influence and equaled Lowell Mason and George Webb in contributions to music education in the United States.[41]

Following the Civil War, Johnson established twelve music conservatories throughout the United States,[42] which included the Seneca Academy in Ovid, New York, (where William E. Bates was listed as treasurer), Miami Conservatory of Music in Xenia, Ohio, and Madison, Indiana, where Bates also was an officer. Bates also served as principal at the Central Indiana Conservatory of Music, where he brought significant musical and managerial expertise to the school.

Boston was a leading city for musical development in nineteenth-century America, and A. N. Johnson was part of the city's vibrant musical scene. According to H. Wiley Hitchcock, although New York City may have been the performance center for the cultivated musical tradition, "undoubtedly Boston was the ideological center."[43] Johnson had assisted Lowell Mason in the development of Boston's public school music program. He also assisted Mason, who served as choirmaster and organist at Park Street Church in Boston, later succeeding Mason in this

The Central Indiana Conservatory of Music. // Bartholomew County
Historical Society

prestigious position. In 1840 Johnson also became the conductor of the
Boston Academy of Music's Juvenile Chorus. He was a crusader for
choral music when Lowell Mason turned his attention to congregational
music. Jacklin Bolton Stopp's research has contributed to rediscovery
of A. N. Johnson's importance in nineteenth-century American music.
She wrote:

> "He was famous in his own day—the teacher of George F. Root and
> Theodore Presser; the founder of several conservatories of music;
> composer of hundreds of hymn tunes and anthems; the compiler of
> music books for common schools, church choirs, and singing schools;
> the writer of books on music theory and choral methodology; the ed-
> itor of music periodicals; and an indefatigable conductor of musical
> conventions, normals, and institutes held in various part of the United
> States."[44]

Benjamin Hutchins' army experiences, extensive travels, and music
teaching experience throughout the country had brought him into con-
tact with exceptional people. He used his contacts to recruit nationally

esteemed, capable musicians to come to Columbus, a town of less than 5,000 people in the Midwest. The desire to bring quality to the community became an identifying characteristic for all development in the future of Columbus. Quality music and musicians came to town; the "cultured" east coast was imported in many ways—this was truly amazing for the heartland.

Artemas Nixon Johnson was one of the fine musicians Hutchins brought to Columbus, and he presented an organ program at the Christian Chapel early in February 1876. By the middle of February, Johnson was conducting a singing school at the church for about fifty scholars.[45] His efforts were well-received, and his musical fame was, no doubt, increased by his organ performance at the Christian Chapel. People were enthusiastic about the efforts of Hutchins and Johnson. A letter to the editor of *The Evening Republican* from a Bloomington, Indiana, resident stated that there was a desire for Hutchins and Johnson to offer "such a convention" someday in Bloomington.[46]

Author's Perspective: Indiana University had been established in Bloomington (about forty miles from Columbus) in 1820, and music courses were offered beginning in 1893. However, there was no department of music until 1910, and no school of music until 1921. Thus, Columbus was very forward-thinking in establishing a permanent school for formal music education. By the time of E. Wayne Berry's Columbus musical leadership (c. 1938 and after), he and First Christian Church's choir cooperated in some significant musical ventures with the Indiana University School of Music under Dean Robert Sanders. Elsie Sweeney, early benefactor of Wayne Berry, was also a key benefactor of Indiana University's burgeoning music school. Today, IU's powerhouse music school, re-named the Jacob's School of Music in 2005, has around 1,500 students and an international reputation for musical excellence. It remains one of the largest music schools in the country.

Therefore, by the spring of 1876 Hutchins had cultivated enough public enthusiasm to bring a more permanent form of music education—a conservatory—to Columbus. City fathers were delighted with his accomplishment, but the citizens of Madison, Indiana, were dismayed over the loss of what had been a successful music school in their community.

Central Indiana Conservatory Leadership, Facilities, and Curriculum

Hutchins sealed the deal and secured financial support for the conservatory by sponsoring a concert at the Christian Chapel in May 1876, in which he and Professor William E. Bates performed vocal and instrumental music.[47] Z. T. Sweeney (colorful, influential preacher at the Christian Chapel) and Dr. Hogue (another influential man of the community) were present at the concert to explain how the proposed school was to be managed. The Christian Chapel was filled, local citizens were given opportunity to speak, and people were asked for financial commitments.

Excitement was high, financing was secured, and a contract was signed with Samuel Hege (builder, owner of a successful lumber company, and member of the Christian Church) to complete a building for a music conservatory by the following September—a rather ambitious deadline. Columbus' movers and shakers of the day brought music education to town with great fanfare through establishing the Central Indiana Conservatory of Music.

Samuel Hege's building was specially designed for the conservatory and was considered "one of the most attractive buildings in the city, situated in a beautiful campus filled with ornamental trees." The c. 7,000 square-foot facility was completed in time for the fall term.[48] It was thirty-six feet by sixty-five feet, included nine rooms and a hall on the first floor, eleven rooms and hall on the second floor, and a concert hall thirty feet by sixty feet on the third floor. A special item of interest was the pipe organ in the main practice hall which was powered by a Bachus Water motor. This water-powered instrument was considered quite advanced for 1876.[49]

Samuel Hege //
Bartholomew County
Historical Society

The Central Indiana Conservatory of Music offered its first music classes in September 1876, with approximately sixty students. Within a few years the school achieved an excellent reputation as students came from Pennsylvania, Wisconsin, West Virginia, Mississippi, as well as Indiana. Notable names among school leadership the first year included several members of the Christian Chapel, plus Benjamin Hutchins, Z. T. Sweeney, Joseph I. Irwin, and Samuel Hege.[50] Administrative officers, faculty, and trustees listed in the *Illustrated Historical Atlas of Bartholomew Co. Indiana 1879* included the following:[51]

OFFICERS
A. N. Johnson, President
Z. T. Sweeney, Vice President
W. E. Bates, Principal
Mrs. W. E. Bates, Lady Principal

H. H. Shull, Treasurer
T. R. Scarll, Secretary

FACULTY
W. E. Bates, Advanced Piano and Organ, Chorus Conductor
Mrs. W. E. Bates, Advanced Voice Culture and Church Music
H. H. Shull, Harmony and Musical Theory
Mrs. Kate Branham, Intermediate Piano and Voice Culture
Miss Rachie R. Ebright, Primary Piano and Thorough Bass
Otto A. Schmidt, Brass and Stringed Instruments in Orchestra Department, and Leader of Orchestra
Will E. Bates, Jr., Violin and Cornet
Louise Johnson (A. N. Johnson's daughter, subjects taught unknown)

TRUSTEES

Joseph I. Irwin	Col. S. Stansifer
Dr. F. M. Mothershead	W. B. Wallace
A. Dalembert	Dr. O. W. Hogue
Col. J. A. Keith	W. J. Lucas
Samuel Hege	Gideon Shultz
Rev. A. Parker	

The *Illustrated Historical Atlas of Bartholomew Co. Indiana 1879* provides further interesting information about the facility:

> *"The upper story is a pleasant concert hall, where examinations, rehearsals, recitals, and concerts of the Conservatory are held. The other stories are taken up with practice and recitation rooms, each room furnished with piano, organ, or such apparatus as may be needed. The Conservatory is lighted throughout with gas and is supplied with water from the Holly Water-Works of the city. The pedal organ is operated by a water motor, so that those who practice upon it need not be annoyed by the presence of a blower."[52]*

William E. Bates (dates unknown)

Daily management of the Central Indiana Conservatory was under the leadership of the principal, William E. Bates. He had been associated with A. N. Johnson and was a graduate of Johnson's Seneca Academy of Music in Ovid, New York; later he was listed as Seneca's treasurer. Bates had also been principal of Johnson's Academy of Music in Madison, Indiana, before Hutchins enlisted him to come to Columbus. In addition to his education at Seneca Academy, Bates had received additional training at Hartsville College, a United Brethren School, only a few miles from Columbus, established in 1850.

Music was an important part of the Hartsville curriculum; the school became Huntington University in 1897. Central Indiana Conservatory of Music personnel listings indicate that the entire Bates family (father, mother, son) all had key involvement. Benjamin Hutchins had sought and secured quality for the music school. Many students came to study at the conservatory because of the fine reputation of William and Jennie Bates. Unfortunately, additional knowledge of William and Jennie Bates seems to have been lost.

The philosophy behind the formation of A. N. Johnson's conservatories was quite consistent with what Benjamin Hutchins had in mind for a school in Columbus. Johnson's schools were designed to produce finely trained church musicians and also to meet the needs of those who desired to be private teachers, public school music teachers, or parlor musicians.[53] It was as important to Johnson to develop Christian character as it was to develop musical talent. Students were expected to attend church regularly on Sundays and chapel services each morning. It did not take long for the Central Indiana Conservatory of Music to establish a fine reputation and draw students from several states.

The class system of the conservatories of Europe was the mode for the conservatory. "It cannot fail to produce the highest possible results," according to the *Illustrated Atlas of Bartholomew Co. Indiana 1879,*[54] which also reported:

> *"The regular course of study is especially adapted to those desiring a complete and thorough education in music at the least expense and in the shortest possible time. It comprises one theoretical study, including the rudiments of music, thorough bass, harmony and composition, in regular order, and any two practical studies (or instruments) the students prefer, or are best suited to him. Singing is usually taken as one of the practical studies, unless the student evinces but little or no talent in that direction."[55]*

> *"In each study classes of from two to six are graded according to the course; the student, on entering, is examined as to his knowledge, progress and ability, and assigned to the grade or class to which he belongs. As the classes of each study meet daily, the student receives about one hundred and fifty lessons of instruction and criticism during the term, or about six hundred lessons during the school year. The practice is all done in the Conservatory building."[56]*

The school year ran from September to June, with four terms of ten weeks each. Following the close of the school year, a normal course was offered, as "one of the most efficient and comprehensive short courses of musical instruction that has ever been invented."[57] Free scholarships to the full normal course were offered to each county in the state, preferably to "one lady and one gentleman."[58] The county superintendent of public instruction issued certificates to those who completed the normal course.

The conservatory had a very successful beginning, and within a year Benjamin Hutchins must have felt things were going smoothly enough for him to dispose of his interest in the school, passing it on to William E. Bates. *The Evening Republican* indicates that the conservatory would be run by the firm name, Bates and Shull.[59] H. H. Shull was also music theory teacher and treasurer of the conservatory.

Benjamin Hutchins returned to partnership with John B. Cobb in the music store where they had previously worked together. However, Hutchins was not sitting idly by with music in Columbus. He used his influence to invite music teachers throughout the state to attend a meeting which resulted in the establishment of the Music Teachers' Association of Indiana (later known as the Indiana Music Teachers' Association).[60] This organizational meeting was held at the Central Indiana Conservatory of Music, June 27-29, 1877. Hutchins had participated in a preliminary meeting in Indianapolis in May 1877.[61]

The Indiana Music Teachers' Association is the oldest state music teachers' association in the United States.[62] William Bates served as one of the early presidents of the state association. A. N. Johnson and the entire faculty of the Central Indiana Conservatory were present for the state organizational meeting, which also was crucial to the progress of the Music Teachers' National Association (MTNA).[63] One of A. N. Johnson's students, Theodore Presser (noted musician and music publisher in his own right), laid the groundwork for MTNA in 1876 and is regarded as the national founder of the organization.[64]

Benjamin Hutchins, Artemas Nixon Johnson, William E. Bates, and Theodore Presser were all early leaders in American public school music education. Like Lowell Mason, with whom Johnson had worked in Boston, all helped the making of music, the performing of music, and the teaching of music become more enriching and more acceptable in nineteenth-century American culture. Mason may have received fame and recognition as the "father of American music education" because he successfully introduced music into Boston's public-school curriculum;[65] but, as we unearth past clues, we see influence of the day's trends—remarkably in Columbus, Indiana—a remote area compared to the elite cities which grew into influential urban musical centers.

Two Musical Paths—Then and Now

At this time in American history there were two distinct musical pathways: the vernacular (popular) tradition and the cultivated (classical) tradition. Vernacular tradition was not driven to establish institutions; it grew in a generative, natural way, drawing from spirituals, folk songs, gospel, and revival hymnody. A. D. Fillmore's singing school had fostered this popular path as far back as 1855 in Columbus. However, it could be said that simply offering normals and singing schools laid the groundwork for more formal music education to come.

B. M. Hutchins, although contributing to vernacular developments through singing schools and normals he had led, allowed his personal experience (especially his lack of formal music education) to influence development which, in a way, bridged the two paths. His personal musical emphasis shifted more to the cultivated pathway by establishing the conservatory. Both the vernacular and cultivated paths grew at an amazingly rapid pace throughout the nineteenth and twentieth centuries, culminating in a vast wealth of music traditions in the nation's melting pot. Columbus was part of the merging of both vernacular and cultivated musical traditions.

Other Music Conservatories in the USA

American music educators established conservatories to promote the cultivated European fashion. At least six quite notable conservatories preceded the founding of The Central Indiana Conservatory of Music in Columbus.[66] The Oberlin (Ohio) Conservatory was established in 1865. Peabody Conservatory of Music in Baltimore was founded in 1857 (although classes were not offered until 1868 because of various hurdles, especially the Civil War). Four other distinguished conservatories were all established in 1867: New England Conservatory and Boston Conservatory (both in Boston), Cincinnati Conservatory of Music, and Chicago Academy of Music. The Central Indiana Conservatory of 1876 was not far behind some very impressive institutions.

Artemas Nixon Johnson had studied in Europe. Lowell Mason had travelled and lectured throughout Europe in 1837 (and found himself somewhat amazed at his fame across the ocean). Therefore it was natural for the European model to be implemented by Benjamin Hutchins and brought to

Columbus, as he successfully engaged influential experts who dedicated themselves to the Central Indiana Conservatory of Music. The six eminent conservatories mentioned above had been pioneered only about a decade earlier. That the small community of Columbus had the foresight and resources to pursue the demanding cultivated musical pathway speaks to excellent leadership, vision, and wealth of those who founded it. Studying the establishment of all pioneering conservatories yields fascinating points of comparison and distinction.

Cultivating Music Outside Church

In nineteenth-century America, moderate-to-large second-floor rooms were created as theaters in commercial buildings. These rooms accommodated musical, theatrical, and dance shows, and other types of lectures and public meetings. The terms "theater" and "opera house" were used somewhat interchangeably. Often, moveable chairs were used for audiences, leaving space for orchestras. Some stages were elevated, but some were on the same level as the audience. First floors of such buildings were occupied by various businesses which supported productions on their second stories. With this information in mind, we can approach the establishment of theaters and opera houses in Columbus. Francis J. Crump had built an opera hall in 1872 (not to be confused with the "new" Crump Theatre, built by his son, John S. Crump. Both Crump venues are covered in chapter four.)

John George Schwartzkopf (July 27, 1835- February 10, 1909) was born in Wissgoldingen, Germany, and came to America in 1851 (age 17) to escape compulsory military training.[67] He arrived in Columbus in 1859 (following short stints in Cincinnati, Newbern, and Taylorsville). Upon arrival, he built a wagon factory and became very successful, even hiring a blacksmith. Although Schwartzkopf was extremely successful as a businessman, he was also an avid lover of music, especially opera. Besides a beautiful, mansion-like home, he constructed (more correctly created) an opera house on the second floor of his building on Jackson Street, the first floor of which was a saloon.[68] It is unlikely he was able to perfectly re-create opera as he knew it from his native Germany, but he tried.

According to a March 10, 1880, article in *The Evening Republican*, Schwartzkopf began to remodel and refitted his theater into a "first class opera house."[69] He wanted to imitate the Park Theater in Indianapolis, with slightly smaller dimensions, but containing six wings and dressing rooms below, an orchestra pit with railing and an entrance under the stage. Schwartzkopf secured architect's plans from Buber and Miller (who had built the Park

Theater in Indianapolis) to guide the remodeling of his opera house. A variety of productions were advertised in the newspaper beginning in November 1880, and the remodeled venue was used not only for road shows, but also for home talent productions, public meetings and other special events. The Salvation Army conducted "rousing rounds of speeches and hymns."[70]

G. Chester Kitzinger, in a 1971 newspaper article, urged saving the Schwartzkopf Opera House. He cited childhood memories of then 92-year-old Frank Quick,[71] who recalled performing at the age of nine in a play based on Mother Goose Rhymes. Quick, Kent Cooper, and Joe Sweeney (Z. T.'s son) were the Fiddler's Three, Milton Reeves played the part of a little crying boy, and M. O. Reeves, John I. Cobb, and W. J. Beck were part of the Tabernacle Quartet that sang. How interesting it is to imagine the involvement of community members in musical and theatrical endeavors apart from those we normally associate with their names.

The heyday for the Schwartzkopf lasted until about 1900, though various programs were presented until around 1920. Public entertainment at this point could be sophisticated—or not—or a combination of both. As late as May 15, 1920, a music and athletic show featured Miss Bernadine Niehaus, ballet dancer; Elise Kitzinger and Ida Edinburn, sopranos accompanied by Miss Louise Mason (all ladies were highly respected, "proper" musicians), along with Joe Walters and Howard Wiggam, boxers, and other athletes of "proven ability."[72] This is quite an interesting combination of talents for a variety show.

The Schwartzkopf Opera House was one of at least five theaters in Columbus, active into the early 1900s. The Pallas Theater was on the second floor of the St. Denis Hotel, but it burned in 1883.[73] The Orpheum Theater was home to both vaudeville and early motion pictures; it was later renamed the American Theater, then the Rio Theater, before closing in 1958.[74] Crump Opera Hall (mentioned above) was a popular venue for several years. However, it burned, and Francis decided not to reopen.[75]

The best-known theater—still to come—would be the Crump Theatre built by John S. Crump (Francis' son) in 1889. The new Crump Theatre contributed greatly to cultural offerings in the community. It was a well-equipped venue for staging any type of show. Many of the most prestigious touring productions appeared there.[76] (More information about Crump Opera House and new Crump Theatre appears in chapter four.)

Continued Programming at The Christian Chapel

Meanwhile, various kinds of musical programs—not necessarily religious in nature—continued to be presented at the Christian Chapel. On Saturday,

July 7, 1877, the Donnell family presented a concert at the church.[77] The Ladies Sewing Society sponsored a benefit concert February 20, 1878, which featured a "traveling show."[78] Another program involving "some of the best musical talent in the city" was advertised for May 8, 1878.[79]

An exceptionally ambitious musical undertaking was reported by *The Evening Republican* during 1877.[80] Professor W. Byron Rice from the Boston Conservatory of Music had conducted a program known as the "Oration of Queen Esther" in Indianapolis, and the newspaper reported he was going to bring it to the Presbyterian church in Columbus. It seems that Rice trained local singers for the production and sang some of the major solo roles himself. He presented "Esther" about fifty times and used thirty costumed young ladies in the performance.

In October 1877 he returned to Columbus to produce an oratorio called *Belshazzar's Feast* (no composer's name given) at the Christian Chapel. The production involved the church choir, Professors Bates and Bergen with string players from the conservatory, and Amasa Cobb as the organist. Both biblical productions may have been staged versions of Handel oratorios. The cultivated tradition—east coast culture—had arrived in the Midwest. Boston Conservatory became known for innovative musical programming, and such programming made its way to Columbus.

Rehearsals, Worship, and Children's Music

Newspaper articles also gave information about music to be performed in Sunday worship services at the Christian Chapel. Choral services were regularly planned for Sunday evenings.

Dr. J. P. Scott was a physician during the 1870s and took an active part in church and community musical activities. He was president of a newly formed Harmonic Society in November 1877.[81] (Amasa Cobb was a member of the executive committee.) The Harmonic Society and the church choir often announced rehearsals to be conducted in Scott's office.[82] Perhaps he recruited more community musicians by not practicing at the church, but it does seem strange to rehearse in a doctor's office.

For at least two morning services in December 1877, *The Evening Republican* listed titles of music in church services. On December 22, the choir sang "Mighty Jehovah" in the morning and "Father, O Hear Us" (a work rehearsed for six weeks, containing four soprano solos) in the evening.[83] (No composer's names appear in newspaper articles until c.1890.) For Sunday, December 29, the newspaper listed the morning anthem as "Make a Joyful Noise," and the evening anthem was to be a repeat performance of "Father, O Hear Us." The morning organ voluntary was listed as "Adagio" and the evening selection as "Larghetto." Unfortunately, again no composer's names were listed.

In October 1878 a children's concert was presented at the Christian Chapel, directed by Benjamin Hutchins. The program was reviewed in the newspaper, and Hutchins was praised for his fine work with young children. It was reported that before the end of the concert, a motion was made, seconded, and unanimously carried to request Hutchins and the children repeat the concert in a couple of weeks. This brief account gives us insight into how things were done in those days. The newspaper reported an admission price of ten cents per person was charged.[84]

An amusing term was applied to music of the Christian Chapel when an article appeared in *The Christian Standard*, printed in Cincinnati, Ohio, and then reprinted by *The Evening Republican* on February 23, 1878.[85] The article was written by D. P. Henderson, who had just finished preaching a revival meeting at the church, in which there were ninety-nine additions to the congregation. Henderson praised every aspect of the congregation and noted that the music was "extra fine."[86] What would "extra fine" mean in today's newspaper?

Z. T. Sweeney (1849-1926), Flamboyant and Effective Preacher

Musical and all other developments at the Christian Chapel took a major step forward when Z. T. Sweeney became the preacher in 1872. He has already been mentioned for his leadership in starting the conservatory, but his influence was profound and far-reaching in a multitude of manifestations.

At twenty-two, Zachary Taylor Sweeney arrived in Columbus to inquire about the pulpit vacancy at the Christian Chapel. He called on the congregation's most prominent member, Joseph I. Irwin, to apply for the position. Z. T. (as he was always known) was greeted at the Irwin front door by Linnie, Irwin's twelve-year-old daughter. Sweeney was so taken by the young girl that he vowed he would marry her some day. Irwin arranged a trial sermon, and on January 1, 1872, Sweeney became minister of the congregation. He began his ministry with the stipulation that he could live with the Irwin family—a bold initiative, but very consistent with his personality. No doubt, he wanted to be closer to young Linnie and proceed with his planned courtship.

The Irwins reluctantly consented to Z. T.'s living arrangement. It was not long before Sweeney broached the subject of marriage to Linnie with her parents.

Tabernacle Christian Church of Columbus with pastor, Rev. Z. T. Sweeney. // Bartholomew County Historical Society

Naturally, the Irwins protested, but Z. T. persisted. Sweeney proved himself to be a very successful preacher and won the approval of the Irwin family to the point where they consented to let Linnie marry Z. T. once she turned sixteen. Therefore, on March 10, 1875, two weeks after her sixteenth birthday, Linnie Irwin became Mrs. Z. T. Sweeney. Truth is stranger than fiction.

Linnie Achieves Her Own Place

To the casual observer it may have appeared that Linnie and Z. T. were unsuited to each other. He was ten years older and a poor man; she was wealthy and accustomed to a house full of servants. At the time of her wedding, she had never even combed her own hair.[87] Nevertheless, Linnie was a great asset to her husband's ministry throughout her life. Because she was free of household responsibilities, she went calling with him during the day. She also taught a men's Sunday school class for many years. Her father enlarged the family home so his daughter and her new husband could still live under his roof following their year-long honeymoon in Augusta, Georgia. It became tradition in the Irwin-Sweeney family well into the mid-twentieth century that several generations live together. At the time of Joseph Irwin's death in 1910, the mansion housed three generations of Irwins, Sweeneys, and Millers.

Linnie's musical impact was profound and long-lasting. She studied piano at the Central Indiana Conservatory of Music in addition to her extremely busy life as a minister's wife, mother to Nettie (born July 5, 1876), Joseph (born Oct. 14, 1880), and another daughter, Elsie (born July 8, 1888). Linnie's approach to music was very serious. We will see her love and serious pursuit of music passed on and lived out in the lives of her children, especially daughters Nettie and Elsie. Linnie, Nettie, and Elsie brought tremendous musical accomplishment and recognition to Columbus.

Unfortunately, Linnie and Z. T.'s only son, Joseph Irwin Sweeney (named for Linnie's father) drowned, at age nineteen, on August 13, 1900, while swimming in the White River near Columbus. Joseph, preparing for his senior year at Butler University, was popular, well-respected as a scholar, athlete, and singer. He possessed a fine voice and was the first president of his college glee club.[88] Only a couple of months before his death, Joseph's solo performance for the Music Teachers' Association meeting had elicited praise in the newspaper.[89] It was a tremendous blow to the family and community when he died so suddenly and tragically; condolences from far and near showered the family.

Ironically, Joseph's grandparents had invited many guests to their home for a golden wedding anniversary celebration.[90] In a strange turn of events, the evening became a wake—mourning the passing of an outstanding young man, rather than celebrating the fiftieth anniversary of his grandparents. Nevertheless, the family persevered, demonstrating their deep faith. Linnie taught her men's Bible School class to honor the memory of Joseph; she also emphasized—as tribute to Joseph, with brother W. G.'s full support—that Cummins Engine Company be dedicated to helping young men develop skills for profitable careers. Linnie and Z. T. were resilient, generous, and together with W. G. they planned strategically for their family's influence. They were worthy recipients of Joseph I. Irwin's legacy.

Z. T. Sweeney's ministry at the Christian Chapel was successful by any standards, and it lasted until 1898, when he was named "pastor emeritus."[91] Many in the community referred to him as Elder Sweeney or simply Z. T. The congregation numbered approximately 200 when he first came to preach. Attendance increased rapidly and doubled by 1877, even though Z. T.'s ministry was interrupted occasionally by extended preaching tours around the country. The Christian Chapel of 1852 seated about 450 but was severely overcrowded by 1876. For special revival meetings it was not uncommon for the auditorium to be full a half-hour before services, and one hundred to two hundred people had to be turned away.[92]

Therefore, at the conclusion of a Sunday service in 1877, Sweeney had the doors of the Christian Chapel locked and announced that no one would leave until $10,000 had been received to start construction of a new building. He possessed leadership ability and charisma to initiate this project—only one year after helping the community raise significant funds to build the music conservatory. Of course, it did not hurt that Z. T. was the son-in-law of a highly-respected, very wealthy man in town—yet he possessed his own unique, amazingly powerful persona. Money was collected, and soon the new building was constructed. Although Z. T. Sweeney's fund-raising efforts may have been somewhat unorthodox, he became famous as a speaker for church dedications and as one who could motivate people to pay off church mortgages.

Z. T. Draws Worldwide Attention

It is fascinating to pause this narrative and recall more of the remarkable life of Zachary Taylor Sweeney. His ministry brought national attention to the congregation, which numbered over 1,000 by 1898. In addition to his role as powerful and popular preacher, Z. T. was appointed by President Benjamin Harrison (good friend of his father-in-law) as consul-general to Turkey from 1889–1891. While he and his family lived in Constantinople, he was also judge of the United States Court. In 1899 Sweeney was chosen to be commissioner of fisheries and game for Indiana and served in that capacity for twelve years. He was a popular speaker at Chautauquas and was under contract with the Redpath Chautauqua and Lyceum Bureau for twelve years. Sweeney was honored with a Doctor of Law degree from Butler University, where he was also a director.

He was a member of the Victoria Institute of London and the Institute of Christian Philosophy of New York. He served as president of the American Christian Missionary Society; and, as chairman of the commission on foreign relations of the Christian Church, he was sent to Russia in 1913 to survey conditions for missionary work contemplated by the society. (A brief reference to his trip appears in *The Evening Republican*.[93] It indicates Russians were enthusiastic about evangelistic possibilities, yet very soon cataclysmic events transpired—World War I and the Russian Revolution—which greatly altered the course of history and thwarted missionary work.)

Sweeney wrote several books and articles for religious publications. He truly connected Columbus with a much larger world through his varied life's work and far-reaching ministry. These important connections were developed even further by his heirs in generations to come.

Columbus Thrives

Columbus grew and thrived in every way. Businesses were established and grew quickly. Beautiful new homes were constructed. The ornate and expensive City Hall was completed in 1874 and is still in use today; it cost $250,000, which was considered an exorbitant amount for the time. The Central Indiana Conservatory of Music got off to a great start and became well-known beyond Indiana. With funding secured for a new building through the efforts of Z. T. Sweeney, the Christian Chapel began to construct a sumptuous sanctuary in February 1878. The congregation moved in one year later—in February 1879 (a short time by the standards then). One month before the move, it was renamed Tabernacle Church of Christ. The church could seat almost one thousand people, and it included a fine pipe organ.

A New Organ for Tabernacle

The organ was originally built by John G. Marklove of Utica, New York, for Fourth Presbyterian Church of Indianapolis.[94] However, it was too large to fit in the Presbyterian church's new building and was taken by Messers. Wm. H. Clark & Co. of Indianapolis in exchange for a smaller organ.[95] Clark completely rebuilt and improved the organ before Tabernacle purchased it. The two-manual instrument with a black walnut console was thought to be the largest organ in the state, outside Indianapolis.[96] The newspaper published its stop list and reported: *"The voicing is well-done, and the rare variety of combinations afforded by this noble instrument will doubtless be a source of just pleasure to the Christian congregation for years to come."*[97]

Tabernacle Church of Christ's new building was considered "one of the most handsome church edifices in southern Indiana and is said to have cost $23,000."[98] It was on Lafayette Avenue (then Mechanic Street) directly across from the Irwin home, which Joseph had greatly expanded. *The Christian Standard* described the building in detail and pronounced the acoustics, arrangement for choir, and organ as excellent.[99]

Tabernacle's new building provided increased musical possibilities—for congregation and community. Several special services were held as part of the dedication of the structure. Concerts were presented on February 4, 7, and 10, 1879, and featured musicians from the church and community, as well as a guest conductor and organist.[100] On February 9, 1879, Isaac Errett preached the dedicatory address in a service which also included several musical selections. Many of the dedicatory events drew audiences of more than 1,000.

Author's Note: Isaac Errett was a speaker of national reputation. He was closely associated with Walter Scott, Thomas Campbell, and Alexander Campbell—all leaders in the Restoration Movement. In 1881, after President James A. Garfield was assassinated, Errett preached Garfield's funeral. It is quite likely Errett was a close friend of Joseph I. Irwin and Z. T. Sweeney. Isaac Errett's grandnephew, Edwin R. Errett, assisted E. Wayne Berry by editing responsive readings for Christian Hymns, *published in 1945.*

In early January 1879, singers from the community were invited to participate in concerts at the new Tabernacle, and they met and rehearsed at the old Christian Chapel.[101] About forty singers rehearsed throughout January. Professor and Mrs. Bates from the conservatory assisted with preparations for all dedicatory concerts, although they were not yet on staff at the church. W. C. Giffe of Indianapolis was guest choral conductor. *The Evening Republican* carried several articles about the dedicatory concerts and printed the program for February 7, 1879.

Frank R. Webb of Lima, Ohio, was guest organist for all dedicatory concerts. The newspaper reported that Webb was "pleased with the organ."[102] Amasa Cobb, who had served as the regular church organist for some time, also performed in the series of special concerts.

All of the dedicatory programs received praise in newspaper accounts. *The Evening Republican* also reported Giffe and Webb were impressed with the quality of women's voices in Columbus.[103] Both guest musicians were surprised "at the number of fine piano players and vocalists" in the city and indicated that the music education in Columbus was superior for a town its size. The newspaper credited the local conservatory as a contributing factor in fostering excellent musicianship in Columbus.[104]

Webb, himself, contributed to music education during his stay in Columbus by offering an organ matinee for children.[105] Admission was ten cents
per child and fifteen cents per adult. The program, no doubt, included how
the pipes created musical sound, and demonstrated tonal capabilities of the
exceptional instrument. There were admission charges for all the special
concerts associated with the dedication, and net proceeds from the series
totaled $250–a tidy sum for the day.[106]

Dedicatory services and concerts were certainly splendid, noteworthy
events, presented for the entire community, not merely for the Tabernacle
congregation. Such programs represented another flowering of amazing
sounds in a Midwestern town.

Community Musical Activities Continue

Some ambitious musical performances were planned for the Columbus
community in 1879. Amasa Cobb announced plans to produce *H. M.
S. Pinafore* at the Pallas Theater and hire either the Indianapolis Opera
House orchestra or an orchestra from Cincinnati for the performances.[107]
The comic opera by Gilbert and Sullivan had only recently been premiered
in London on May 25, 1878, and was, therefore, quite an innovative work
for Columbus to perform.[108] Unfortunately, fire destroyed the theater, and
plans for the production were eventually dropped.

There appeared to be a good spirit of cooperation among the churches in
Columbus, and the organ at the Tabernacle was used for various occasions.
Mr. Siegfried, organist at Dr. Humphries' church in Louisville, was engaged
for a lecture-recital.[109] Frank M. Ketcham, organist at Fourth Presbyterian
Church in Indianapolis, assisted in this lecture-recital, which was sponsored
as a benefit concert for the local Presbyterian congregation.[110] The Presby-
terian church used the concert to help raise money for a new ten-stop Estes
Cabinet organ. (This reference likely refers to an "Estey" organ.)

On April 9, 1879, the Mendelssohn Quintette Club of Boston gave a concert at Tabernacle "for the benefit of the Church."[111] This elite East-Coast
ensemble was the pioneer chamber music organization to travel throughout the United States. One of its founders, Thomas Ryan (1827-1903), a
great admirer of Felix Mendelssohn, decided to name his ensemble for
the revered composer. Although the quintet normally performed in larger
cities, they were attracted to Columbus by the reputation of the conservatory. General admission was fifty cents; reserved seats were seventy-five
cents. The quintet was praised in the newspaper following a second performance, and the community hoped to schedule them again in the fall.[112]

A program of music and recitations by the "Summers children," assisted by other "youngsters from Columbus" was presented at the Tabernacle in April 1879. One interesting selection on the program was a duet for harp and organ which featured Amasa Cobb as organist and Charles J. Pence, a high school student, as harpist.[113] Admission was also charged for this concert: adults, fifteen cents; children, ten cents.

A somewhat controversial program was given at Tabernacle on July 25, 1879.[114] Teachers of the conservatory directed fifty little girls dressed in various bird costumes in a program entitled "The Musical Charade or Contest of the Birds." Admission was more expensive for this children's concert: general admission was twenty-five cents, and reserved seats were thirty-five cents. It seems that some trustees from the church objected to the movements of the children, which they labeled as "dances," and they frowned on such presentations. Objections were printed in the newspaper, as well as a defense by William Bates, who denied that the children danced. The movements were probably what we call choreography today.

An unusual concert was presented at Tabernacle on May 16, 1879.[115] Blind Tom was an African-American virtuoso pianist from Georgia, who caused quite a sensation in the community. He played brilliantly and was probably autistic, but many felt he was exploited by the Bethune family of Columbus, Georgia, who were supposed to protect his welfare. Blind Tom Wiggins had been born a slave in 1849 on the Wiley Edward Jones plantation in Harris County, Georgia. He was the first African American to perform at the White House—at age eleven—for President Buchanan. Reportedly, he had a repertoire of more than 7,000 popular songs, hymns, spirituals, and classical selections and could play anything he heard. It was said he practiced up to twelve hours a day.[116]

Tom had appeared in Columbus, Indiana, in March 1873, at Crump's Opera House (a smaller venue—not the "new" Crump Theatre).[117] Although people supported his concerts, many felt he was simply being used to make money for his family and was not valued for his amazing musical talent.

From the completion of the Tabernacle, the building was used for community-wide activities besides musical concerts. High school graduation exercises and graduation exercises for the Central Indiana Conservatory of Music were held there. James Whitcomb Riley, celebrated Hoosier poet, presented a program at the church on March 1, 1880.[118] The church was also the location for some rather unusual congregational events. At Christmas time in 1879, they sponsored performances of a "secular" cantata, Santa Claus, to benefit children of the Sunday School.[119] William Bates and Benjamin M. Hutchins organized this production. The variety of Tabernacle programming in general, and musical programming in particular, throughout the 1870s and 1880s is truly remarkable.

Taking Time to Assess

As the 1870s and 1880s progressed, the citizens of Columbus had much to be proud of and thankful for. Following the Civil War, renewed efforts to build the community were enthusiastically pursued, despite occasional financial downturns. (There was a terrible financial storm in 1873.) The East-Coast gilded age found its own Midwestern flare. Joseph I. Irwin and John S. Crump had fiscally sound banks, and these two entrepreneurs enabled others (the Cobb family, William H. Donner, Col. James Keith, William Ruddick, many of the Reeves family, to name a few) as forward-thinking participants in economic and cultural progress.

Classical music was not forgotten, even though people may not have fully realized its growth. John George Schwartzkopf brought his love of opera to Columbus, although opera productions he loved did not dominate the type of programming his Columbus opera house presented.

As churches grew, they built fine sanctuaries which boasted the latest provisions for organs and choirs. Z. T. Sweeney's positive leadership was exercised nationally and internationally—well beyond the walls of Tabernacle Church of Christ. Gas lighting was beginning to provide safer illumination—although fires were still ever-present threats. The waterworks ensured safe drinking water, and sewers were still to come. Streets were starting to be paved. Interurban transportation to nearby thriving communities was a boon to all, but horses, carriages, and wagons were everywhere. Farming was very successful, yet a growing business district developed along Washington Street and adjacent blocks of Third and Fourth streets.

Skilled craftsmen could be secured for almost any imaginable project. Public schools were thriving and providing instruction in music—Benjamin Hutchins' influence had been strong, even as the Central Indiana Conservatory of Music brought European and East-Coast culture to the Midwest through Artemas Nixon Johnson, William and Jennie Bates, and many exceptional visiting performers. Singing Schools and normals waned; vaudeville and minstrel shows continued, and classical music found its place, too. The last three decades of the nineteenth century were a golden age for all aspects of life—who could imagine anything better to come? Columbus had great foundations on which to build; it was known as a progressive community throughout the state and beyond—distinctive for many reasons—especially music.

1. "History," *A Century of Christian Progress 1852-1952*, Commemorating the 100th Anniversary of the first permanent church building of the Christian Church, Columbus, Indiana, [N. P.]. This booklet was compiled by an unnamed committee for the centennial celebrations.
2. Ibid.
3. Ibid.
4. Hugh Th. Miller, "Tabernacle Church of Christ, Columbus, Indiana, History: 1829-1940," p. 3.
5. "History," A Century.
6. Miller, "Tabernacle," p. 4.
7. Ibid.
8. James Deforest Murch, *Christians Only* (Cincinnati, Ohio: Standard Publishing, 1962), p. 106.
9. "History," *A Century.*
10. Ibid.
11. Miller, "Tabernacle," p. 6.
12. Obituary of Joseph I. Irwin, *The Evening Republican*, August 16, 1910, p. 1.
13. Laura Fawcett Arnold, "Singing School," *Ye Olden Tyme* (May 1897, p. 56; rpt. Columbus, Ind.: *Bartholomew County Historical Scrap Book No. 10-#339*, 1980.
14. Ibid.
15. Joseph I. Irwin, *History of Bartholomew County, Indiana, 1888, Vol. I* (Columbus, Indiana: Avery Press, 1976), p. 253.
16. Richard Harold Gemmecke, "W. G. Irwin and Hugh Thomas Miller: A Study in Free Enterprise in Indiana" (Ph.D. Dissertation, Indiana University, 1955), p. 2.
17. Ibid., p. 3.
18. Ibid., p. 4.
19. Ibid., p. 6.
20. Ibid., p. 9.
21. "Joseph I. Irwin," *History of Bartholomew*, p. 253.
22. Obituary of Joseph I. Irwin, p. 8.
23. Gemmecke, p. 11.
24. Ibid., p. 12.
25. James Small, "The Old Days, The Old Ways and the Old Friends" (A History and Souvenir of the Christian Churches of Bartholomew County, Indiana and the Church at Nashville, Brown County for the Bartholomew County Christian Missionary Association, 1928), p. 6.
26. "B. M. Hutchins," *History of Bartholomew County Indiana, 1888, Vol. I* (Columbus, Indiana: Avery Press, 1976), p. 252.
27. Ibid.
28. Registry of Members of the Christian Chapel, Columbus, Indiana, Joseph I. Irwin, clerk. [N. P.] (This registry is held in the files of the Irwin Management Company.)
29. Obituary of Joseph I. Irwin, p. 1.
30. Announcements in *The Evening Republican*, October 18, 1877, and November 12, 1877, p. 3
31. *The Republic*, www.therepublic.com. Isaac T. Brown founded The Columbus Republican, a weekly newspaper, in 1872. The first issue was published on Thursday, April 4, 1872. In 1877, the newspaper began publishing six days each week, and in 1883 the name was changed from *The Daily Evening Republican* to *The Evening Republican*. It became *The Republic* in 1967.
32. "City and Vicinity," *The Evening Republican*, February 3, 1876, p. 8, and August 23, 1877.
33. "The Normal Institute," *The Evening Republican*, July 25, 1872, p. 3.
34. "Review," *The Evening Republican*, August 29, 1872, p. 3.
35. "Christmas Eve," *The Evening Republican*, December 26, 1872, p. 3.
36. Ibid.
37. *The Evening Republican*, May 1, 1873, p. 3.

38. Laura Long, "Horse and Buggy Ways," *The Evening Republican*, December 12, 1957, p. 12.
39. Ibid.
40. Ibid.
41. Jacklin Bolton Stopp, "A. N. Johnson, Out of Oblivion," *American Music,* Vol. 3, No. 2 (Summer, 1985), p, 154.
42. Telephone conversation with Jacklin Bolton Stopp, July 31, 1988.
43. H. Wiley Hitchcock, "The Cultured Tradition," *Music in the United States: A Historical Introduction, 2nd Edition.* Englewood Cliffs, New Jersey, 1974, p. 131.
44. Jacklin Bolton Stopp, "Out of Oblivion," American Music, Vol. 3, No. 2, p. 156.
45. "Professor A. N. Johnson," *The Evening Republican*, February 13, 1876, p.8, and February 17, 1876. [N. P.}
46. Ibid.
47. "The Indiana Conservatory of Music," *The Evening Republican*, May 11, 1876.
48. Ibid.
49. "Conservatory," *The Evening Republican*, November 30, 1876.
50. Laura Long, "Horse and Buggy," p. 4.
51. "Central Indiana Conservatory of Music," *The Illustrated Historical Atlas of Bartholomew Co., Indiana.* Chicago: J. H. Beers & Co., 1879, p. 13.
52. Ibid.
53. Ibid.
54. Ibid.
55. Ibid.
56. Ibid.
57. Jacklin Bolton Stopp, "A. N. Johnson, Out of Oblivion," p. 156.
58. "Central Indiana Conservatory, " p. 13
59. *The Evening Republican*, July 12, 1877. P. 1.
60. Official Program, Indiana Music Teachers' Association, Twenty-Third Meeting at Columbus, June 26,29, 1900, p. 2.
61. Ibid.
62. Ibid.
63. Jacklin Bolton Stopp, "A. N. Johnson," p. 162.
64. MTNA website indicates Theodore Pressor as the Founder in 1876.
65. H. Wiley Hitchcock, "The Cultured Tradition," p. 131
66. Ibid.
67. Laura Long, "Schwartzkopf's Opera House," historicalcolumbusindiana.org.
68. Ibid.
69. Ibid.
70. Ibid.
71. Ibid.
72. Ibid.
73. Ibid.
74. Ibid.
75. The Crump Theatre, Historic Columbus, Indiana, historiccolumbusindiana.org/jscrump.html.
76. Ibid.
77. "City and Vicinity," *The Evening Republican*, July 5, 1877.
78. "City and Vicinity," *The Evening Republican*, February, 19, 1878.
79. "City and Vicinity," *The Evening Republican*, May 6, 1878, p. 3.
80. Survey of Announcements in *The Evening Republican*, September 3, 1877 through October 18, 1877.
81. "City and Vicinity," *The Evening Republican*, November 27, 1877.
82. "City and Vicinity," *The Evening Republican*, December 15, 1877.
83. "Churches," *The Evening Republican*, December 22, 1877, p. 3.
84. "Little Folks' Concert," *The Evening Republicann*, October 10, 1878, p. 3.
85. D. P. Henderson, "Columbus," *The Evening Republican*, Saturday, February 23, 1878,

p. 1 (reprinted from *The Christian Standard* Cincinnati, Ohio: Standard Publishing Company).

86. Ibid.
87. Robert Earl Reeves, A Biography of Z. T. Sweeney (Master of Arts thesis, Butler University, 1959), p. 17.
88. "Joseph Sweeney," *The Evening Republican*, August 14, 1900, p. 4.
89. *The Evening Republican,* July 23, 1900, p. 4.
90. *The Evening Republican*, August 15, 1900, p. 2.
91. Reeves, A Biography, p. 17
92. Ibid.
93. *The Evening Republican*, July 7, 1913, p. 1.
94. *The Evening Republican*, January 15, 1879, p. 4.
95. "The New Organ in the Tabernacle," *The Evening Republican*, February, 5, 1879, p. 4.
96. *The Evening Republican*, February 6, 1879, p. 4.
97. Ibid.
98. Hugh Th. Miller, Tabernacle Church of Christ, Columbus, Indiana, History 1829-1940, p. 6.
99. *The Christian Standard* (Cincinnati: Standard Publishing Company, February 15, 1879), p. 52.
100. *The Evening Republican*, January 10, 1879, p. 4.
101. Dedication, p. 4.
102. *The Evening Republican*, February 6, 1879, p. 4
103. Ibid.
104. Ibid.
105. Ibid.
106. *The Evening Republican*, February 11, 1879, p. 4.
107. *The Evening Republican*, February 14, 1879, p. 4.
108. www.operaamerica.org.
109. *The Evening Republican*, February 26, 1879, p. 4.
110. *The Evening Republican*, April 12, 1879, p. 4.
111. "A Genuine Musical Treat," *The Evening Republican*, March 31, 1879, p. 4.
112. Ibid.
113. *The Evening Republican*, April 11, 1879, p. 4.
114. Survey of articles in *The Evening Republican* from July 22, 1879, through July 26, 1879.
115. *The Evening Republican*, May 14, 1879, p. 3.
116. www.blackpast.org/african-american-history/wiggins-thomas-blind-tom-1849-1908.
117. "Blind Tom at Crump Opera House," *The Evening Republican*, March 13, 1873, p. 3.
118. *The Evening Republican*, March 1, 1880, p. 4.
119. *The Evening Republican*, December 2, 1879, p. 4. D. P. Henderson, "Columbus," *The Evening Republican*, Saturday, February 23, 1878, p. 1 (reprinted from *The Christian Standard* Cincinnati, Ohio: Standard Publishing Company).

Chapter Four: Ups and Downs in the Musical World

When things go well, people tend to continue as if there is no turning back on progress. Such moving forward accompanies a musical mindset, too. Most Columbus development through the end of the nineteenth century was positive; however, fire, financial downturns, and personnel changes created setbacks. Yet, despite problems, musical development did move forward in Columbus.

Capitalizing on community cooperation and success, several churches in town joined in the summer of 1879 to conduct a Sunday School Convention at Tabernacle Church of Christ.[1] Many local ministers and musicians took part; preachers from Protestant churches in the community supported the convention, and even the local Rabbi addressed the gathering. Besides many guest speakers, Isaac Errett, nationally-respected preacher and writer from Cincinnati, returned once again to speak. The Tabernacle choir performed, Miss Mollie Quick sang "Sweet Bye and Bye," Benjamin Hutchins led singing, and one of the afternoon speakers was J. H. Rosencrans, "one of the prominent singers of the Christian Church."[2] *The Evening Republican* published the following statement at the conclusion of the convention:

> *"Does Honorable J. C. Robinson, president of the convention, deal in 'taffy' or did he mean it when he said that the members of the Tabernacle congregation ought to be happy, because they had one of the finest churches, one of the best preachers, one of the best organs, and one of the best financiers in the State? Guess he meant it."*[3]

Amasa Cobb (1851-1886)

Amasa Cobb was very active as choir director, organist, trombonist, and even became director of the city's cornet band.[4] He taught piano and organ, and *The Evening Republican* reported he was "re-elected to the position of organist at Tabernacle for another year."[5] This terminology seems a bit odd today, and maybe it was simply a vote of confidence. But at age twenty-five, in February 1880, Cobb resigned and moved to Chicago and became a bookkeeper. Perhaps he just needed a change, or like so many musicians, required a steadier source of income.

The church honored its departing organist with a concert featuring "the best musical talent in the city."[6] The newspaper reported that for his last Sunday services, Cobb played Mendelssohn's "Wedding March" and Wilson's "Shepherd Boy." Mendelssohn's "How Lovely are the Messengers" and Handel's "Sound the Timbrel" were also listed for the service; these were probably choir anthems Cobb accompanied.[7]

Amasa Cobb often returned to Columbus to visit family after moving to Chicago, and his name appeared in various newspaper accounts of events at Tabernacle Church of Christ. Unfortunately, his health began to fail, and he returned to Columbus in 1886, where he tragically died at the age of thirty-one. Cobb must have been loved and well-respected as a person and musician, too.

Records do not clearly indicate whether Cobb was paid as organist at church. During his last six months as organist, the "official board" of the church elected Benjamin R. Irwin as "leader of the choir."[8] It is not known whether he was paid, either. Benjamin R. Irwin's father (also named Benjamin) was the charter member of the congregation who had given a portion of his farm more than sixty years earlier for the congregation's first building. Despite tremendous change, Irwin family members continued their involvement in music; Amasa Cobb's mother was Joseph I. Irwin's sister.

William and Jennie Bates (no dates available)

William Bates replaced Cobb. Bates was well-known to the congregation because of close ties to the music conservatory. Evidently the recent dispute with church trustees over "dancing" in one of his children's productions did not keep him from being considered for the position. Mr. and Mrs. Bates were Methodists, and Benjamin Hutchins used his influence to persuade Professor Bates, as he was always known, to take the job of organist at the Tabernacle. Once again, Benjamin Hutchins' efforts resulted in positive musical benefits. No doubt, Bates was also enticed to take the organist position because of the fine, new organ at Tabernacle.

Sunday, February 29, 1880, was William Bates' first Sunday as organist at Tabernacle Church of Christ. The newspaper reported that he planned to play works by Handel for the evening service.[9] Mrs. Jennie Bates did not begin her employment with the congregation until January 1883. When she was hired, *The Evening Republican* reported:

> *"Mrs. W. E. Bates has been employed to take general charge of the music in the Christian church in connection with the professor. All*

members of the old choir are requested to meet immediately after Sunday School tomorrow afternoon for the purpose of reorganization."[10]

Although we are not sure if predecessors Amasa Cobb and Benjamin R. Irwin were paid for leading music at church, we know for certain that William and Jennie Bates were paid for their musical services at Tabernacle. From their time onward, records indicate the congregation hired musicians. The long history of paid organists and choir directors is remarkable, in and of itself. Many congregations would be hard-pressed to know who their musicians were throughout the preceding century.

By March 1883, the choir drew praise from the newspaper, which stated that the Tabernacle choir showed "marks of steady improvement under the energetic leadership of Professor and Mrs. Bates."[11] William and Jennie Bates brought a new level of professional musicianship to the leadership of the church's music program. Both were well-known as church musicians and educators. Townspeople had already witnessed the number of students who came from several states to study under their direction at the conservatory. Their combined leadership created a win-win situation for music at the church and in community.

Horizons Expanded

During the years of William and Jennie Bates' musical leadership at the church, several conservatory programs were held at Tabernacle. Some involved members of the church choir participating with conservatory students and faculty. One program of this nature was presented on January 18, 1887,[12] when Jennie Bates conducted the combined church and conservatory choirs, Professor Bates accompanied at the organ, and Professor A. H. Graham sang some of the bass solos for a performance of Henry Farmer's Mass in B flat. (It is noteworthy that this performance was conducted by a woman.)

The newspaper helped to educate the people of Columbus by printing an article on the history, structure, and Latin text of a concert mass.[13] A "large and appreciative audience" attended the performance. Besides Professor Graham, soloists included M. T. Reeves (well-known businessman), John I. Cobb (brother of Amasa), Miss Nerva Tomes, Miss Vickey Burks, Miss Clara Cox, Mrs. Maggie Irwin, Miss Pearl Haines, and Miss Lou Belle Wilson. The review of the concert stated "there has never been in our town a chorus more thoroughly drilled and disciplined, though we have had conductors here of national reputation."[14] Wow— Jennie Bates hit a home run.

Newspaper coverage also reported that the combined forces of the church and conservatory would soon start on Mozart's 12th Mass and Handel's *Messiah*.[15] These were ambitious plans for future presentations, and they indicate the rapid and effective growth of both conservatory and church programs.

Author's Note: Henry Farmer (1819-1891) was an English violinist and composer who was basically self-taught. He had played in the orchestra for the premiere performance of Mendelssohn's Elijah *and composed his* Mass in B Flat *in the style of Haydn and Mozart in 1839 at the age of twenty. The Brown & Stratton Company first published the mass in 1844. Farmer wrote several instructional "tutors" (how-to-books) for teaching orchestral instruments. Such tutors were probably used for instrumental instruction at the Central Indiana Conservatory of Music.*[16]

Columbus Music Stayed Current

Several other musical concerts and services at the church were given excellent newspaper coverage during Professor and Mrs. Bates' leadership at the church and conservatory. A choral service was presented in May 1880, and in 1885 the Tabernacle was "packed above and below" to see "a rendition of the Japanese Wedding" from *The Mikado* by Gilbert and Sullivan.[17] Costumes were secured from Chicago, and the performance was given on Christmas night. Benjamin Hutchins performed one selection. Gilbert and Sullivan had just premiered *The Mikado* in London during 1885; it was a newly composed English operetta. This undertaking was quite remarkable for the time; it demonstrates the knowledge and capabilities of the Bateses and talent of the community. Midwestern Columbus stayed current with music from the world-stage—amazing.

Tragedy Strikes

Musical progress at the Central Indiana Conservatory of Music under the Bateses continued through most of the 1880s. Newspaper articles indicate that Professor Bates had been very active publicizing and recruiting for the conservatory. He spent nearly $1,000 on advertising and circulated up to forty thousand catalogues to prospective students in 1879.[18] His efforts paid off. Student attendance increased to the point two new rooms were added for instructional space.[19] The school grew at a rapid pace, and positive reviews gave credit to the conservatory for its fine impact on music in the community.

Unfortunately, one of the severe tragedies for the city and particularly the musical community occurred in November 1887, when the conservatory was destroyed by fire. The beautiful building depicted in the *Illustrated Historical Atlas of Bartholomew Co. Indiana 1879* burned to the ground.

Tabernacle Church of Christ had benefitted from the conservatory in a special way because William and Jennie Bates provided musical leadership for both institutions. The Bateses combined musical forces from church and school to present some outstanding programs; it had been a win-win situation—until the fire. Following destruction of the conservatory building, a more modest structure was constructed, but proverbial dominoes were beginning to fall. Besides down-sizing the conservatory facility, a scaled-back program of instruction was offered—to no avail. The tragic fire and scaled-back instruction combined with a severe economic downturn in the 1890s to thwart rebuilding efforts, and the conservatory was soon disbanded.

By March 1, 1890, the deacons of the church terminated William Bates' services.[20] No doubt, disbanding the conservatory was partially to blame, but so was the severe economic depression. Sadly, little is known about William and Jennie Bates after they left Columbus and moved to Martinsville, Indiana, later in 1890. The Bates family had contributed greatly to the entire community's musical development, and they had helped establish a standard for musical excellence which survived after their departure. Furthermore, the prominent role of Jennie Bates with her husband demonstrates a forward-thinking approach to the leadership role of women in music and ministry. All in all, despite the tragedy, Columbus was still well-ahead of its time in many musical ways.

Regroup and Go On

My research has indicated the Central Indiana Conservatory of Music was a much more important institution for musical development in Columbus and the surrounding area than people realize. Sadly, its former existence is hardly known at all today. However, the conservatory put Columbus prominently on the musical map for more than a decade. More importantly, it helped set a standard for what people in the community came to expect from music education and performance. Benjamin Hutchins, Joseph I. Irwin, John S. Crump, and J. George Schwartzkopf continued to bring quality to Columbus in their musical endeavors, and even though there were economic setbacks, musical advancement still occurred. Very soon, the ambitious and capable Irwin-Sweeney-Miller women would take decisive leadership roles for musical development, following the legacy Jennie Bates left.

Tabernacle Church of Christ maintained its leadership in music for worship and community. Although, during some rough financial times in 1890 the board of deacons made a proposal to reduce expenses by eliminating two staff members—the solicitor/secretary and the organist (Arthur Mason)—the proposal failed to receive support, especially from the eldership which included Joseph I. Irwin and Benjamin Hutchins. The finance committee was instructed to borrow money to meet the necessary expenses of the church.[21]

The church's pipe organ seemed to have been the source of frequent trouble and, thus, frequent repairs and expenses. While Professor Bates was in charge of the music, he was also requested to make all repairs to the organ. He agreed to do so for an additional $30 per year in 1889. William and Jennie Bates received salaries from the church through February 1890. He was paid $100 per year, and she $50. To help put these figures in perspective, it should be noted the entire offering receipts for a year at this time would have totaled approximately $3,000.[22]

Further insight into music and financial matters of the times concerns the organ. Isaac T. Brown had installed a twenty-two-inch Bachus water motor in the basement of the Tabernacle in July 1879 to run the organ. Deacons' minutes of 1888 stated that the new janitor, Josiah Quick, would be expected to pump the organ a reasonable amount of time for the organist (William Bates) to practice.[23] The water-powered motor required manpower for operation.

Arthur Mason Builds a Varied Career and Re-establishes Standards

Following a brief term as organist by Minnie Keith, the church hired Arthur W. Mason in 1891 with the salary of $5 per week.[24] Mason was twenty-five years old; it seemed to be a tradition at the church to hire young organists.

Arthur Mason was born in Lexington, Ohio, on November 19, 1866. He was a child prodigy and played both organ and piano in his church and at local dances when he was just eight years old.[25] Mason participated in a local band led by an exceptional circus band leader, and the experience served him well. At age fifteen he toured the Midwest as organist with a family of bell ringers. Although his musical education was quite unorthodox, he established a fine musical reputation in a short time. Mason had enlisted in the army and was a member of the 14th and 17th regimental bands before being honorably discharged.[26] From 1886 to 1891 Mason was musical director for three theatrical road companies, and distinguished himself in theater music before becoming involved in church music. The position at Tabernacle was his first church position; however, he continued involvement in church music with various congregations for more than forty years, later serving Third Christian Church in Indianapolis.[27]

Arthur Mason also taught music in public schools, and in 1891 he became supervisor of public school music in Columbus.[28] He continued to supervise music in various Indiana school systems until 1920, when he became associate director of Louisville Conservatory of Music for one year.

Mason returned to Indiana in 1926 to become director of the Indiana College of Music and Fine Arts in Indianapolis. The school became part of Arthur Jordan Conservatory of Music, which Mason led from 1926-1932 (during E. Wayne Berry's enrollment as a student). The conservatory was established in 1928, when benefactor Arthur Jordan purchased it and combined it with the Metropolitan School of Music and Indiana College of Music and Fine Arts. In 1951, Arthur Jordan Conservatory became affiliated with Butler University.[29] It is more than a little confusing to keep history, development, and combination of these schools straight.

Mason was deeply involved in music education throughout his life, and he certainly wore many musical hats, taking on the musical mantle of Benjamin Hutchins. He served as president of the Indiana Music Teachers' Association for two years, president of the National Conference of Public School Music Supervisors in 1915, and was president of the Kentucky Music Teachers' Association in 1925 during his last year of employment in Kentucky.[30] During his Columbus years Mason was very active as a pianist, organist, choral director, piano tuner, teacher of music theory, and director of an orchestra at Crump's Theater—he was very busy and very versatile. He married Minnie Reeves, daughter of A. B. Reeves, on April 27, 1892.

The title of professor was often attributed to Mason while he was at the church, perhaps as a carryover from the days of Professor Bates, or simply because he excelled as an effective leader, administrator, and performer. Years later, Indiana University's Jacobs School of Music established the Arthur W. Mason scholarship in his honor.[31] His fame and musical service had been extremely significant throughout the state, and he certainly made a lasting, positive impact.

On January 30, 1891, the ladies of the Tabernacle sponsored a supper and organ recital by Arthur Mason.[32] For five cents a person could attend the recital, and for an additional twenty-five cents one could have supper before the program. I believe this program was a gesture of welcome from the congregation. He must have performed very well because *The Evening*

Republican reported that the recital received not only applause, but "repeated applause."[33]

It seems Mason must have been serving the congregation in an interim capacity prior to his official employment, since he directed the Tabernacle choir in concert on February 25, 1891–less than ten days after he was formally hired as organist. The concert is notable for at least two reasons. Mason used his theater orchestra (probably from Crump's Theater) of sixteen members to accompany the Tabernacle choir. Also, the program, which was printed in the newspaper, included composers' names.[34] This is the first instance of a program accompanied by a large instrumental ensemble at the church, and it is the first listing of composers' names with composition titles. Mason upped the standards for printed programs, and future printed programs indicate his standards were maintained, even to the present day.

There were other notable developments at the Tabernacle while Mason was employed. Several documents mention a Christian Church Choir Choral Club which presented a program in 1895 under Mason's leadership. This may have been a community choir, and it is reported as the earliest printed record of a musical organization sponsored by the church (not simply allowed to rehearse/perform there); however, no printed copies of the program still exist. There were earlier musical groups which rehearsed at the church, but this organization seems to have had official, on-going status—at least for a while.

In February 1895, Mason received permission to spend $5 each month on the choir. This was presumably the first time money was regularly budgeted for the purchase of music.[35] Mason's administrative and organizational skills made a positive impact on music, not just at church, but also in the community. During his employment at church, his salary ranged from $5 to $7.50 per week during winter months. In the summer of 1899, he was paid $15 per month for June, July and August.

A Committee on Music had been appointed in 1897 consisting of two elders: M. T. Reeves and B. M. Hutchins. Mason was instructed to "confer with this committee at all times." In the same year he was requested to "train a class of boys and girls at least one hour every week in vocal music." From this class Mason was instructed to organize a chorus which would perform at least one selection every Sunday morning.[36] Wow! To modern musicians, it is quite demanding to have a children's/youth choir prepared to perform every week.

Mason continued to serve as organist and choir director with the Tabernacle congregation regularly until at least September 1899, and he may have served intermittently until 1912. Printed records, reports, and historical documents leave some confusion in interpretation. Mason was remembered as a stern, severe man, very demanding in his leadership, whether in the music program of the church, theater, or school.[37] His musicianship was excellent, and his organ playing was characterized by great energy and enthusiasm.[38]

About four months before Arthur Mason died, on September 22, 1955, he wrote a letter to his son reflecting on his busy life more than a half century earlier:

> *"It takes me back further to Columbus. In the first ten years we were in the 1890 depression—tough going, but we were never in debt. By 1900 things began to move and for fifteen years were on the go with school, teaching, church—a steady grind of the same things. Every once in awhile I would get fed up, go to Indianapolis for an afternoon, see a show, and the walls that seemed so high in Columbus melted away when I looked at them from a distance."*[39]

Author's Reflection: The paragraph Arthur Mason wrote to his son prior to his death gives insight into what all busy musicians occasionally feel, no matter where they serve. Furthermore, capable musicians often find themselves performing, conducting, administrating, filling gaps, recruiting, trying to cut corners and save pennies to keep everyone happy. Musical careers are much more demanding than listeners often perceive. Most musicians today can identify clearly with Mason's plight and need to get away at times. His words ring true more than seventy-five years later.

Instrumental Music Developments

As far back as Amasa Cobb, there had been a city cornet band, which Cobb directed until leaving Columbus for Chicago in 1880. This group may have been preceded—or coexisted—with a city band which the newspaper claims was organized before 1843.[40] By 1888, Gary C. Davis organized Big Six band which was a descendent of the earlier city band. Gary C. Davis' father-in-law, Joseph Sheets, led the Sheets Family Band which included Sheets and Davis family members. A photo in *The Republic*, July 7, 1979, pictured this group as it existed in 1912.[41] The Sheets Family Band played together until 1931 and included Clara Sheets Davis and Gary C. Davis, parents of Gary F. Davis Sr. (also pictured). The Sheets Family Band had performed with Buckskin Ben's Wildwest Band. Gary and his wife also appeared on Mississippi and Ohio River showboats. When she was just sixteen years old, Clara Sheets Davis was judged to be the best clarinetist in the state of Indiana.[42] Very impressive.

Gary C. Davis gave up traveling to settle in Columbus and operate a grocery store. But he found time to play in the Columbus Opera Theater (not sure where this orchestra was located). He played a vital role in introducing instrumental band music classes at the old Columbus High School, where he became the first instrumental music teacher.[43] Therefore, he helped lay foundations for important instrumental developments to come, especially through his son.

In 1939 the Sheets Family Band reorganized for a family reunion. For this occasion, Gary F. Davis Sr. (son of Gary C.) played trumpet. He was quite precocious and as a grade schooler organized a thirteen-member orchestra which he conducted![44] At that young age he played with the Columbus High School Band, too, and at one time was the band's assistant music director. He played professionally off and on, but gave up to concentrate on his music store. Later he joined G. Chester Kitzinger's Columbus Symphony and also played in the Seymour Symphony. In both orchestras he played baritone. He quit playing only because he needed to spend more time with his store. He was the father of three sons, Gary Jr., Dan, and Tom, who all followed in their father's musical footsteps. In actuality, there have been eight generations of musicians spanning more than 165 years in this amazingly talented family. The Columbus City Band still exists and performs regularly today.

A Look at Crump Opera/Theatre in Columbus

As Columbus grew and musical endeavors diversified, churches were not always suitable venues for performances. The picture of the pulpit/choir loft area of Tabernacle Church of Christ reveals its limitations for new types of productions.

J. G. Schwartzkopf's opera house has been mentioned (located on Jackson Street, west of the courthouse), and it remained a popular venue until c. 1900, but it became outgrown and outdated. New venues were constructed or adapted from previous buildings. Adaptations involved name changes, as well as remodeling of older structures.

Not every facility used for musical or theatrical purposes has provided a clear history for us today. Some street names have changed, buildings have been remodeled/renamed, memories may not always be detailed/accurate, and family involvement has to be sorted out among several generations who passed on the same, or similar names. Such is the case with the

GRAND OPENING.

J. S. Crump's Theatre,

OCTOBER 30 AND 31.

Norcross : Opera : Company.

First night in an original interpretation of Chas. Lecocq's Charming Comic Opera,

"The Pretty Persian,"

Or "The Hullah's Bride.

English Libretto by J. W. Norcross, Jr., Lyrics by Matt. C. Woodward. Second night in Auber's master-piece, the fascinating comic opera

"Fra Diavolo,"

Tickets now on sale at Joe Weller's drug store. Buy early and avoid the rush. Reserved seats

$1.00, 75 and 50 Cents

Top: The Crump Theatre, 1889. **At left**: A flyer promoting opening night at the Crump Theatre. **Above**: John S. Crump. // Bartholomew County Historical Society

Crump and Keith families and venues associated with their names. Below is information to bear in mind.

The Crumps

Francis J. Crump I (1801-1881) helped establish First National Bank in Columbus, and was a theater lover. He had two sons, Francis T. Crump II (1837-1917), and John Smith Crump (1843-1920). John Smith Crump had a son Frank (Francis) Crump III; and Ross Crump (president of the Bartholomew County Historical Society for twenty years) had a son, Francis Crump IV. There were a lot of Crumps to identify—it gets very tricky to do so. Crumps were movers and shakers in various Columbus developments. Francis J., although much older than Joseph I. Irwin, was a banker at the same time Irwin was getting started in banking.

The Keiths

Along with the Crumps, the Keith family made significant contributions to the Columbus community. The family was headed by Isham Keith Sr. (1808-1891), who had two sons, Col. John Alexander Keith (1832-1910), and Lt. Col. Squire Isham Keith. Jr. (1838-1862), who was killed during the Civil War. Col. John Alexander Keith was an attorney who had served as a trustee of the Central Indiana Conservatory of Music. He had built an arcade in 1871 providing space for various businesses; Keith Hall, on the second floor, was used for musical concerts and various programs.[45] Keith and Crump names became associated with stage productions, and researchers since have had to sort out what was what.

Francis J. Crump I contracted in 1872 for a new opera hall to be built. The new building was on the northeast corner of Washington and Walnut streets. The newspaper reported the street floor was being rapidly fitted up with stores, one of which was J. B. Cobb's Books and Stationery. Once the structure was built, Francis hired Hege, Mathew & Co. in July to finish the woodwork, hopefully by September, but September turned into October. On October 26, 1872, *The Evening Republican* reported

> *"Crump's new Opera Hall (not theatre) is just about completed.[46] Its appearance has been much improved by the beautiful frescoing of the ceiling. Mr. Reynolds, the artist, and his assistant have done their work in a manner that reflects much credit on themselves.*

Columbus has now a hall of which none of her citizens need be ashamed, though it is much regretted that Mr. Crump did not build it a little more in the style of an opera house."[47]

The grand opening performance on October 28, 1872, was by White and Turner's Troupe,[48] which must have made a stop in Columbus during their performance tour. When Francis J. Crump's opera house was destroyed by fire some years later, he decided not to rebuild.[49]

Keith and Crump Connection

In 1888, Col. John Alexander Keith was placed in the Indianapolis Insane Asylum. At the time, Keith owed Frank T. Crump (Francis I's older son) $28,000. In order to satisfy the debt, Keith's court-assigned guardian had most of his property sold at auction. The courthouse auction was conducted in January 1889, and John Smith Crump, younger brother of Frank T, acquired the Keith Arcade property for $6,000.[50] John Smith Crump soon hired architect Charles Sparrell to draw up plans and specifications for a theater to be constructed adjoining the south side of Keith's Arcade building. The contracting firm of Keller and Brockman was awarded the construction job on April 22, 1889.[51] Sparrell and Crump worked together in the selection of nationally-renowned theatrical firms that specialized in interior theater design and scenic painting.

During construction of the theater's auditorium, the old Keith's Arcade portion of the building was remodeled. The section underneath the middle arch became the entrance way, and adjacent areas were rented out for businesses; rooms on the second floor were rented out to "day boarders."[52] The words, "Keith's Arcade A. D. 1871," embedded within each arch at the top of the building, were removed and replaced with "Crump's New Theatre."[53] Crump's-New-Theatre opened October 30, 1889, with the Norcross Opera Company of Chicago performing *The Pretty Persian* by well-known French composer Charles Lecocq. The next night, October 31, Daniel Auber's comic masterpiece *Fra Diablo* was presented. Since the poster advertising these two opening operas included mention of an English libretto, it is thought that both operas may have been presented in English,[54] rather than French—still, very high class productions for small-town Indiana.

John Smith Crump's New Theatre was the first "stand-alone" opera house/theater in Columbus, yet it was attached to the previously built arcade, which had been associated with Keiths. It was equipped to present the most up-to-date modern shows, musicals, and operas. The interior was beautiful and elegant, with the lower floor seating as many as 600. It was the first theater in town to be designed according to the needs and demands of the best traveling shows of the day. The size of the stage could accommodate the large hand-painted scenes that were tailored specifically to a particular play.

Some twenty-five years later, On May 6, 1914, a newsreel of the soon-to-be-completed Panama Canal—on August 15, 1914—was shown at Crump Theatre, and this event foreshadowed the future, almost exclusive use of the venue, for motion pictures in years to come. Some call this showing the first motion picture shown in Columbus. With the advent of movies offering synchronized sound in 1929,[55] new Moviephone equipment was installed. The first all-talking movies were shown at the Crump on March 11, 1929, and included *Redskin*, starring Richard Dix, and *That Party in Person*, starring Eddie Cantor. The theater was sold in 1931, and in 1934 a major renovation began. It included a new RCA high-fidelity sound system and a new Vocalite movie screen.[56]

Crump's New Theatre was to play a significant role in Columbus performing arts well into the mid-twentieth century. It was remodeled several times, and the outside facade was modernized in 1941 with stucco to create an Art Deco appearance. The theater almost had its name changed to the Von Ritz because of a contest, but public opinion was opposed to the name change, and it was dropped. Recently, significant updates have been made to the Crump Theatre, recalling its important place in the cultural history of Columbus. It is being restored to become another jewel in the architectural crown of the city.

Turn-of-the Century Musical Situation

Columbus' population had grown to about seven thousand by 1900. It boasted many fine homes, an elegant courthouse, beautiful churches, at least five opera houses/theaters, and had acquired statewide distinction because of its leading families, many of whom were successful capitalists and generous philanthropists. Cultural progress had transformed the community rapidly during the preceding century. Quality of life was exceptional. Pioneer families of the 1820s would not have recognized the city seventy-five years later.

Z. T. Sweeney concluded his formal ministry with Tabernacle Church of Christ in 1898, but his influence throughout the state, and indeed, the world, connected his church and city to a much greater audience. Sweeney's speaking ability and influence were noteworthy, and his heirs inherited many of his exemplary leadership traits.

Music was influenced by new inventions and technology, especially electricity. Electric powered motors, all manner of lighting, amplified sound, and recorded sound were either available or on the immediate horizon. Acoustic music did not go away, but all performing aspects of music were ripe for transformation. Perhaps the last transformation came in church music; however, by the last half of the twentieth century, church music, too, was almost completely transformed. Changes occurred ever so quickly.

Music at Tabernacle Church of Christ

Just prior to 1900, Tabernacle Church of Christ was still a mainstay of musical expression in the community, even with Z. T. Sweeney in retirement. The church had at least two established quartets which were part of the musical scene of church and community. Although it became common for congregations throughout the country to use quartet members as paid section leaders for their choirs, this was not the case at Tabernacle. It may have been the norm in other Columbus churches. Tabernacle's quartets functioned independently from the choir and provided special music for church services, funerals, evangelistic meeting, and other programs in the community.

As early as 1889, the Home Missionary Society of the congregation featured a male quartet which attracted "considerable attention."[57] Members of this ensemble were John Emmons, Will Beck, Milton Reeves, and B. M. Hutchins. Proceeds from their performances helped benefit the work of the missionary society.[58] Eventually John I. Cobb replaced Beck, and later, Will Halsey replaced Hutchins. Norval Hege (who will later be an important personality behind establishing the symphony) started singing with the quartet when another member retired. A mixed quartet was composed of Catherine Newsome Jewell, Milton Reeves, Alex Foster and Beulah Brown. Printed programs in the newspaper indicate Tabernacle's quartets performed for many occasions.

From 1897 through at least 1900, Benjamin Hutchins was chairman of the music committee at Tabernacle. He had expressed some disapproval of the music, especially the children's choirs, during the last few years of Arthur Mason's employment.[59] No doubt, Hutchins was still the strongest advocate for music education at church, as he had also been years earlier in the community. It is also likely he exercised significant influence in the selection of a replacement for Arthur Mason.

William A. Harding

Early in the fall of 1899, William Harding was chosen as Mason's successor at Tabernacle; his title was director of music.[60] Harding was a pianist, and when he played for services, an instrument had to be brought into the sanctuary (whether a grand or an upright, the moving of such an instrument was a huge task). By the beginning of the twentieth century, the piano was becoming much more of a church instrument, even though many thought its connection to bars and dance halls made the instrument inappropriate for church use. Interestingly, this viewpoint did not seem to prevail at Tabernacle. Miss Bertha Lay was hired as organist at the church, and in 1900 she married Will Harding. Piano/organ/marriage issues were settled.

William A. Harding was born in 1873 in Mexico, Missouri.[61] Once again, the church hired a young man; he was twenty-four. He earned bachelor's and master's degrees from Sherwood School of Music in Chicago, studying piano with Xaver Scharwenka, the great Polish pianist and composer; harmony and analysis with Cuthbert Clarkson; instrumentation with Theo S. Evens; and counterpoint, canon and fugue with Walter Keller.[62] He was an extremely well-trained musician.

Before coming to Columbus in 1899, he taught music and did concert work. Harding was a highly respected music teacher and church musician throughout his years in Columbus. In 1917, following the outbreak of World War I, he returned to Chicago as extension department examiner, teacher of ear training and theory, and director normal class for affiliated teachers outside of Chicago for Sherwood School of Music.[63] (The Sherwood school was acquired by Columbia College in Chicago in 2007.)

In Columbus, Harding was head of a branch of Sherwood School of Music and was known for his extensive music library containing over 500 volumes on music history and theory.[64] He was the author of a three-year course in ear training and sight-singing and contributed many articles to *Etude* and *Musician* magazines and other publications. Throughout his Columbus years he taught piano, voice, and music theory. He tuned pianos, and was significantly involved with Tabernacle Church of Christ in various paid and volunteer positions.

On January 9, 1902 (the fifty-year anniversary of the congregation), Harding wrote a letter describing his musical program at church.[65] The letter was sealed in a special box which was not to be opened for one hundred years, but was opened by mistake in 1915. The letter contained a listing of members of an orchestra Harding had organized earlier: William Schnur, violin; Frank Lay, clarinet; Joe Sheets, coronet; Harry Brown, trombone; Orin Gaston, bass; and, Miss Elva Reeves, piano. He mentioned that the orchestra was then under the direction of Fred Doeller. Harding gave the size of the adult choir as forty-five members and mentioned a junior choir of twenty-five.

During the years of Harding's musical leadership, new hymnals were purchased and all song books for use in Sunday School. The earliest hymnal known to have been used by the congregation was entitled *New Christian Hymn and Tune Book*, a selection of hymns and tunes for Christian worship in two parts, published by Standard Publishing Company, Cincinnati, Ohio, 1882. It was compiled and edited by James H. Fillmore (A. D. Fillmore's son), who, like his father, was associated with Restoration Movement congregations. (A. D. Fillmore had conducted a singing school many years earlier for the congregation.) The hymnal was used in Tabernacle's worship until sometime in 1902, when a new hymnal with Fillmore as co-editor was purchased. The new hymnal was entitled *The Praise Hymnal*, a collection of hymns and tunes edited by Gilbert J. Ellis and James H. Fillmore, copyrighted in 1896 by Fillmore Brothers, 119 W. Sixth St., Cincinnati, Ohio. (This is the hymnal pictured in this book, which was given to the author by E. Wayne Berry. It has Joseph I. Irwin's name engraved on the cover and is now part of the Columbus Historical Society collection.)

The full extent of Will A. Harding's musical leadership at Tabernacle Church of Christ from the fall of 1899 through the spring of 1917 is complicated. Minutes of deacon's meetings, elders' meetings, and finance board meetings indicate several personnel changes. One interesting note states Harding was given permission for the Columbus Oratorio Association (which he may have also conducted) to practice in a room at the church building for one dollar per night. Also, Harding recommended that a tent be placed around the organ in the choir loft to protect the organist against the cold while practicing.[66] How interesting. The tent would surely have been cheaper than heating the entire sanctuary, but would it keep fingers warm?

Constant changes in music leadership from 1904 through 1913 did not strengthen the overall music program. Although Hugh Th. Miller's report as president of the board of elders (January 1907) mentioned the fine music of Miss Haggard during the preceding year, by March 1908 the music committee was instructed to find out what could be done to improve the choir.[67] The eldership of the congregation was also in a period of transition by 1913. Strong supportive voices such as Marshall T. Reeves and Hugh Th. Miller were raised on behalf of the music program, but the long-term consistent guidance of Joseph I. Irwin had ended with his death in 1910. Furthermore, the positive influence of Benjamin M. Hutchins waned with his failing health during the last two years of his life.

During many ensuing years of overall instability, Will Harding did what he could, serving as elder, and also as a salaried financial secretary and musical director. Z. T. Sweeney—though still an influential voice in church and community—had officially resigned his Tabernacle position in 1898,

Harriet Glanton Irwin died in 1908; Joseph I. Irwin died in 1910; and Benjamin M. Hutchins died in 1918. The old, faithful guard was passing away and it was time for new leadership, especially in music.

Elise and G. Chester Kitzinger

Stability was restored to the musical leadership and programming of the church by the close of Will Harding's ministry. In November 1917, Tabernacle Church of Christ hired Mrs. G. Chester (Elise) Kitzinger (1894-1940) as choir director and soloist.[68] A paid soloist in a Restoration Movement congregation was not the norm, even a century later. Elise Kitzinger was a coloratura soprano who had attended Cincinnati Conservatory of Music. She became a church member and taught many voice students in Columbus. Her salary of $50 per month indicated her ability and reputation in the community, and she maintained the position until November 1919.[69] She was assuming the mantle of Jennie Bates.

In May 1919, Mildred Brown resigned as organist. She was replaced in July 1919 by Miss Louise Mason, daughter of Professor Arthur W. Mason. When Elise Kitzinger resigned as choir director, Louise Mason took over as organist and choir director for a short time, resigning both positions in November 1920. Although very talented, Mason was much less experienced than Kitzinger and was paid just $6 per month—quite a bit less than Kitzinger received for her leadership and service.

Oldest Symphony Orchestra In Indiana Established

George Chester Kitzinger (1894-1977), a Roman Catholic, played an essential role in the development of music at Tabernacle and in Columbus. Kitzinger had studied violin at Cincinnati College of Music under William Morgan Knox, famed violinist with the esteemed Cincinnati Symphony Orchestra for forty years. Kitzinger was from Columbus, and upon graduation from college returned home in 1917. He worked in his family's bakery and began teaching violin.[70] Two churches soon approached him about starting orchestras: first, the United Brethren Church, and in 1918, Tabernacle Church of Christ.[71]

Evidently, the small orchestra Will Harding had organized around 1902 had been disbanded. But it had laid the groundwork for the orchestral concept Kitzinger re-established at Tabernacle. At the invitation of Norval Hege (member of one of the church's popular quartets, a local funeral director, and enthusiastic Sunday School superintendent), people were recruited to restart an orchestra. On April 9, 1918, the United Brethren and Tabernacle orchestras combined to play for a Sunday School meeting at Tabernacle.

By 1920 Kitzinger resigned from the United Brethren orchestra and continued with the Tabernacle orchestra, which numbered approximately thirty players.[72] Norval Hege had the orchestra play for ten minutes on Sunday mornings before Sunday School and also took the ensemble to various cities, including Indianapolis, Winchester, Greenfield, and Louisville to perform for special services. The picture of the inside front of Tabernacle's building does not show much space for orchestral arrangement, either on the main floor or balcony. A great deal of weekly setup and tear down was required for regular musical presentations. Kitzinger's Tabernacle orchestra had a very auspicious beginning, but there was even more to come.

Columbus already had a solid foundation of instrumental talent which had been fostered by the Central Indiana Conservatory of Music decades earlier. Amasa Cobb had directed a city cornet band. The city had some form of a band for decades, directed by Gary F. Davis Sr.'s family members. Kitzinger decided to add the growing number of string players he taught to the city band.[73] The strings and band rehearsed on Sunday afternoons at the Chamber of Commerce, and after working together for a year, presented their first concert as the Columbus Symphony Orchestra on May 17, 1922, at Crump Theatre.[74] In the orchestra's second concert appearance Elsie Sweeney was accompanist and performed a Franz Liszt concert Etude (quite a musical feat). Mrs. Anna Newell Brown, contralto, presented two vocal solos with orchestra, "Pilgrim" and "The Kingdom Within Your Eyes" by Oley Speaks.[75]

Kitzinger conducted forty-six concerts between 1922 and 1954. The Columbus Symphony was the first symphony orchestra in Indiana, preceding the Indianapolis Symphony by eight years.[76] Membership usually numbered about eighty players. Neither regular players nor the conductor were paid, but in the early years a few instrumentalists were hired from neighboring cities. Once again, these dedicated instrumentalists were willing to rehearse and perform wherever and whenever possible—a lot of logistical considerations were necessary to navigate since the ensemble had no permanent performing/rehearsing venue. This was truly a remarkable achievement by extremely dedicated players.

In 1925, seventy-five members of the symphony from Columbus (a city of about 9,000) played in Indianapolis for the state convention of the Indiana Federation of Music Clubs.[77] Sixteen members of the Tabernacle Sunday School Orchestra were members of the 1925 Columbus Symphony Or chestra.[78] G. Chester Kitzinger continued to lead Tabernacle's orchestra during the 1930s, and he assisted as violinist for special Tabernacle choral programs through at least 1936.[79]

The Evening Republican, May 23, 1933, reported a memorable Columbus Symphony program presented at the high school gymnasium. The newspaper declared the concert attended by c. 500 to be the orchestra's "best of it's eleven years' history."[80] All three movements of Saint-Saens' Concerto for Piano and Orchestra, Op. 22, were performed, featuring E. Wayne Berry as pianist. (Naturally, Berry performed the entire concerto from memory; he was twenty-three and, no doubt, had worked diligently preparing the concerto while studying with Ernest Hutcheson at Juilliard.) William Morgan Knox, Kitzinger's famous violin professor from Cincinnati College of Music, came to assist local Columbus string players. The orchestra also performed "Ballet Egyptian" by Lugini, selections from Gounod's opera, *Faust,* and the Fourth Movement of Dvořák's *New World Symphony*.[81] Kitzinger conducted the entire concert, and the audience included attendees from Edinburgh, Indianapolis, Osgood, and Seymour. The program was obviously a huge success, and the orchestra's fame increased.

Another noteworthy symphony concert was reported in *The Evening Republican*, Saturday, Feb. 26, 1949. This was the thirty-eighth symphony concert and was presented in the high school gymnasium. Kitzinger conducted, Mrs. Dorothy Munger (pianist from the Indianapolis Symphony) accompanied, and the violin soloist was Leon Zawisza, concertmaster and assistant conductor of the Indianapolis Symphony.[82] Zawisza performed Lalo's *Symphonie Espanole* concerto. The full orchestra performed works of Mozart, Beethoven, and Mendelssohn. Dorothy Munger had studied with Joseph and Rosina Lhevinne, therefore she and Elsie Sweeney, no doubt, had much to talk about.

Claude C. Smith

In 1921, Claude C. Smith, who played euphonium in the City Band and the Columbus Symphony, took over directing Tabernacle Church of Christ's choir. Smitty, as he was affectionately known, returned from World War I and became a Prudential Insurance agent. Although he was not trained as a musician, he was naturally talented and beloved by all who worked with him; he remained on staff at the church until 1938. Smitty possessed a fine baritone voice and had sung in the choir at the Methodist church, where his wife, Mabel, had been organist. Mabel was an accomplished pianist and organist. The Smith's had been married only a short time when the Tabernacle congregation hired Smitty as director of music.

From time to time, when rearing a family permitted, Mabel Smith served as organist or assistant organist at Tabernacle. Claude Smith was a very likable person, responsible for developing a fine spirit and sense of loyalty among choir members.[83] The choir was characterized by such attributes, even after Smitty's years as director. He was the director in 1925 when fifteen-year-old Wayne Berry started his career as choir accompanist and organist—Smitty not only paved the way for, but also supported young Berry's leadership.

During Claude Smith's leadership, the choir sponsored special programs known as Old Melodies Concerts. Programs for at least two of these concerts still exist (February 23, 1928, and March 5, 1931). The Old Melodies Concerts were very popular and featured the choir in various costumes, performing mostly secular, patriotic, and folk music. Solos, ensembles, and instrumental music were included, too.

Author's Reflection: *As a musician with more than fifty years experience in churches, community groups, and Christian colleges, I never shied away from programming secular music (a term I don't like, but use anyway). Occasionally, I had to justify my selections to skeptical choir members, parents, and audience members who questioned my "liberal" tastes. I replied by stating my philosophy calmly, clearly, and concisely, and we all went on our way. The issue was not worth getting mad about. I smile to see programming in a leading conservative Christian church—more than a hundred years ago—found purpose for music other than worship music and classical music; I suppose you could say I feel "historically vindicated." Professor Berry spoke fondly of Old Melodies Concerts, too. I realize how musical boundaries today have been stretched and tried, and musical programming is NOT as simple as it used to be.*

Music in Columbus progressed with enthusiasm, quality, and variety. It seems each new generation of musicians was able to build on what had been established previously. Challenges and obstacles were met by talented and visionary men and women. Quality leaders were enlisted and supported. Whole-hearted community involvement existed and cooperation among churches, schools, and community organizations benefitted everyone. Columbus, Indiana, was a great place to live and enjoy music.

1. "Sabbath School Convention," *The Evening Republican*, July 30, 1879, p. 4.
2. *The Evening Republican*, July 31, 1879, p. 4.
3. Ibid.
4. *The Evening Republican*, July 8, 1879, p. 4.
5. Ibid.
6. *The Evening Republican*, February 6, 1880, p. 4.
7. *The Evening Republican*, February 21, 1880, p. 4.

8.	*The Evening Republican*, October 15, 1879, p.4.
9.	*The Evening Republican*, February 28, 1880, p. 4.
10.	*The Evening Republican*, January 6, 1883, p. 4
11.	The Christian Social, *The Evening Republican*, March 10, 1883, p. 4.
12.	The Evening Republican , January 19, 1887, p. 4.
13.	"Farmer's Mass in B flat," *The Evening Republican*, January 10, 1887, p.4.
14.	"Farmer's Mass in B flat," *The Evening Republican*, January 19, 1887, p. 4.
15.	Ibid.
16.	Henry Farmer Mass in B flat
17.	"Sunday Service," *The Evening Republican*, May 15, 1880, p. 4; The Evening Republican , December, 26, 1885, p. 4.
18.	*The Evening Republican*, Saturday, April 26, 1879, p. 4.
19.	Ibid.
20.	Deacons' Meeting Minutes, February, 17, 1890, p. 61.
21.	Deacons' Meeting Minutes, August 10, 1891, p. 92.
22.	Deacons' Meeting Minutes, January 3, 1894, p. 56.
23.	Deacons' Meeting Minutes of December 3, 1888, p. 28; announcement in The Evening Republican, July 31, 1879, p. 4.
24.	Deacons' Meeting Minutes, February 16, 1891, p. 4.
25.	"Arthur W. Mason Musical Scholarship Fund," Jacob's School of Music, music. indiana.edu.
26.	Student's Record, Indiana College of Music and Fine Arts.
27.	"Third Christian Musical Enterprise to be Directed by Arthur W. Mason, *The Indianapolis Star*, September 19, 1932, [n. p.].
28.	Student's Record.
29.	Ibid.
30.	Ibid.
31.	"Arthur W. Mason Musical Scholarship Fund," Jacobs School of Music.
32.	*The Evening Republican*, January 29, 1891, p. 4.
33.	*The Evening Republicann*, January 31, 1891, [n. p.].
34.	"Tabernacle Choir Concert," *The Evening Republican*, February 24, 1891, p. 4.
35.	Deacons' Meeting Minutes, February 20, 1895, p. 75.
36.	Deacons' Meeting Minutes, January 4, 1897, p. 98.
37.	Letter from E. Wayne Berry, August 27, 1988, p. 1.
38.	Interview of Josephine Hutchins Schumaker (Benjamin Hutchins' daughter) on August 30, 1988. Mrs. Schumaker compared the energy and style of Mason to Dan McKinley, who was then the current organist.
39.	Letter in files of Bartholomew County Historical Society.
40.	"Sheets Family, Gary Davis Music Makers," *The (Columbus, Ind.) Republic*, July 7, 1979, p. 22.
41.	Ibid.
42.	Ibid.
43.	Ibid.
44.	Ibid.
45.	Iorio, Tamara Stone (2010). Columbus. Charleston, S.C.: Arcadia Publishing. p. 31..
46.	*The Evening Republican*, October 26, 1872, [n. p.].
47.	Ibid.
48.	*The Evening Republican*, October 28, 1872, [n. p.].
49.	www.historiccolumbusindiana.org/jscrump.html, p. 2.
50.	Sechrest, David (2013). *Columbus Indiana's Historic Crump Theatre*. p. 54
51.	*Columbus Indiana's Historic*, p. 56.
52.	Ibid.
53.	Ibid.
54.	www.historiccolumbusindiana.org/jscrump.html, p 4.
55.	"*Columbus Indiana's Historic*, p. 101.
56.	Ibid.

57.   *The Evening Republican*, February, 1, 1889, p. 4.
58.   Ibid.
59.   Elders' Meeting Minutes, September 6, 1897, [n. p.].
60.   Deacons' Meeting Minutes, October 2, 1899, p. 140.
61.   "No News is Good News," *The Evening Republican*, May 31, 1945, [n. p.].
62.   Printed information received from The Sherwood Conservatory of Music, Chicago, Illinois, October 28, 1988.
63.   Sherwood Music School archives collection, digitalcommons.colum.edu.
64.   Henry R. Fish, "Professor Will A. Harding," *Illustrated Columbus, Indiana,* 1915, no publishing information, [n. p.].
65.   This letter is in the archives of First Christian Church library.
66.   Finance Board Minutes, February 2, 1914, [n. p.]
67.   Elders' Meeting Minutes, January 3, 1907, p. 64.
68.   Deacons' Meeting Minutes, December 1917, [n. p.].
69.   Employments Agreement between Mrs. Chester Kitzinger and Tabernacle Church of Christ.
70.   Laura Long, "Horse and Buggy Days, Columbus Symphony: Community Institution and Asset," *The Columbus Republican*, February 11, 1965, p. 1.
71.   "Columbus Symphony Led the Way," *The Columbus Republican*, June 11, 1968, p.4.
72.   Personal notes of G. Chester Kitzinger on file at Bartholomew County Historical Society.
73.   Ibid.
74.   "Columbus Symphony Led," p. 4.
75.   "Ovation Given Orchestra at Concert Close," Second Appearance, *The Evening Republican*, Saturday, February 9, 1924, p. 1.
76.   "Columbus Symphony Led," p. 4.
77.   Ibid.
78.   Comparison of lists of 1925 Columbus Symphony Orchestra personnel (from *The Republican*, November 18, 1970) with 1925 listing of Tabernacle Church of Christ Sunday School Orchestra personnel (from publicity handout card, dated 1925, in church library). Sixteen Tabernacle players were listed in the symphony orchestra.
79.   Survey of existing programs from 1927 through 1936 in First Christian Church library.
80.   *The Evening Republican*, May 23, 1933, p. 1.
81.   Ibid.
82.   "Steinway Concert," *The Republic*, Monday, October 13, 1997, p. 8.
83.   "Music," *A Century of Christian Progress 1852-1952*, Commemorating the 100th Anniversary of the first permanent church building of The Christian Church, Columbus, Indiana, [n. p.].

Chapter Five: E. Wayne Berry's Early Years

One of the most significant musical developments in Columbus, Indiana, occurred during the 1920s when E. Wayne Berry entered the community's active musical scene. Berry's interaction with influential people and world-class musical talent brought significant fame and achievement to the community. Eventually, Berry, himself, became a conduit for bequeathing music to a host of worshippers, worship leaders and students through his teaching in three institutions of higher education. Berry was extremely active in Columbus music for over forty years.

E. Wayne Berry was born on October 13, 1909, in Hillsboro, Indiana. His parents, who had been members of the Hillsboro Church of Christ, joined Tabernacle Church of Christ upon moving to Columbus in 1910.[1] His family members were active participants at the church throughout their lives.

Berry's first piano teacher, his mother, started teaching him when he was nine years old. She had to make him practice. Shortly after mastering Beethoven's Minuet in G, Berry began studying piano with Miss Louise Mason (Arthur Mason's daughter), choir director and organist at Tabernacle Church of Christ.

Following a short period of study with Louise Mason, Berry began to study with Miss Jessie Kitchen, organist at First Presbyterian Church in Columbus.[2] Kitchen taught several students, and in many respects, was ahead of her time as a piano teacher. She included music theory and composition sessions on Saturday mornings for groups of her students. Those who met at her house were seated at tables which were provided with large staves and silent keyboards. Basic triads, sevenths, and some details of composition were taught using such aids. Students enjoyed composing pieces, many of which were later performed in recitals. Kitchen was remembered for instilling great enthusiasm for music in her pupils. No doubt, her impact made a lasting impression upon Berry, who taught music theory to many college students decades later.

When Berry was ready for more advanced instruction, he began studying with Miss Eleanor Beauchamp, a teacher from Arthur Jordan Conservatory of Music in Indianapolis, who came to Columbus one day a week to teach piano.[3] She helped young Berry decide to pursue a career in music. At this point in his life he wanted to become a concert pianist. (Elsie Sweeney also reinforced this dream.) Throughout high school, Berry studied with Beauchamp and maintained a rigid practice schedule of three to four hours a day. The high school administration even permitted him to leave school during the last period each day in order to practice. Beauchamp presented Wayne Berry in a public recital at Tabernacle on May 28, 1927.[4]

Columbus was a very musical town in the "Roaring '20s." Besides the efforts of G. Chester Kitzinger and his orchestra, Gary F. Davis' City Band, the Crump Theatre, and programs of churches, there was also the Ladies' Matinee Musicale, which sponsored regular concerts featuring local talent and guest musicians. The Musicale sponsored many of Berry's recitals, and through its concerts he was able to accompany most of the featured singers and violinists. One of the young singers he accompanied was Frances Pearce, who later became his wife.

Another influential music teacher during Berry's high school days was Miss Ida Edinburn.[5] She was a graduate of New England Conservatory of Music and had studied with Oscar Saenger (1868-1929), noted, innovative voice teacher of the day. She was a soprano and supervisor of music in the Columbus public schools, and nurtured Wayne's desire for a musical career through classes in music theory and music appreciation. Such classes acquainted him with a large repertoire of music from all periods of history. Besides benefiting from Edinburn's classes in school, Berry also benefited from practicing on her Steinway piano at home. He remembers struggling with Chopin's f-Minor Fantasy on her Steinway. Berry also had access to Elsie Sweeney's Steinway grand for practice; therefore he had excellent instruments available for developing technique and honing his craft.

One day in 1923, Edinburn asked Berry to play an offertory on the organ at First Presbyterian Church, where she was choir director. Although he had never played an organ before, he knew *Etude* magazine published a couple of organ pieces in each issue along with piano music. Therefore, he played an organ piece chosen from *Etude* for the offertory. He must have played well and passed his "audition," because the next day Edinburn asked him to become organist at First Presbyterian Church. He was just thirteen years old. Berry recalled the rashness of youth causing him to accept the position, which became a fast-paced learning experience.

He was grateful to the congregation for enduring what he felt must have been a painful experience for them while he learned to play. He said his sight-reading was so bad in those days that he had to practice the hymns a week in advance.[6] (At some point in his development, Berry became an excellent sight-reader.) Nevertheless, this experience at First Presbyterian was the beginning of his lifelong interest in playing the organ. Talented, visionary women of Columbus—beginning with his mother, and continuing with Louise Mason, Jessie Kitchen, Ida Edinburn, Eleanor Beauchamp,

—

Elsie Sweeney, and culminating with Nettie Sweeney Miller—all paved the way for Berry's notable musical successes.

In 1925 E. Wayne Berry accepted the position as organist at his home congregation, Tabernacle Church of Christ—with little experience. He also accompanied the choir led by Claude Smith. To the outside observer Berry may have appeared to be a poor choice as organist, especially for a congregation with a tradition of fine organists and exceptional instruments extending back to Amasa Cobb, William Bates, and Arthur Mason. And, the congregation numbered about one thousand people.

However, the church was well-acquainted with Berry's natural talent and self-discipline. Furthermore, influential Irwin-Sweeney-Miller family members (particularly Nettie Sweeney Miller) recognized his potential, as well as the possible long-term benefit for the church. The risk to them was nonexistent. Berry's first formal organ training began shortly thereafter, in Indianapolis, at Meridian Street Methodist Church, under Mrs. Myra Clippinger.[7]

In 1927 Berry graduated from high school and continued as organist at Tabernacle church after enrolling at Arthur Jordan Conservatory of Music in 1928. His 1929 employment contract with the church specified a salary of $12 per week, providing he played for morning and evening services, as well as rehearsals. (Four dollars per service or rehearsal was to be deducted for every service or rehearsal missed.) Berry was not allowed to give private lessons on the organ or let anyone else use the instrument. He was also expected to play for funerals of church members without extra pay. Practicing on the organ was limited to preparation of music for Tabernacle church services. However, he was given one month's vacation with full pay.[8] These firm guidelines help underscore the type of discipline Berry later came to expect from his college students at the Cincinnati Bible Seminary.

Off to Juilliard

During Berry's high school and college years, Elsie Sweeney's influence on his musical career was at its peak. Although she was approaching forty (well beyond the age most musicians study seriously—or for personal fulfillment), she still made extended trips to New York to study piano, attend concerts, and visit friends. Her appreciation, love, and discipline for music was truly remarkable. And she was quite talented. She was well-aware of The Juilliard School because of her previous piano study with Josef and Rosina Lhevinne in Berlin (who joined the Juilliard graduate faculty in

1924), and Ernest Hutcheson, Austrailian piano virtuoso, who also joined the Juilliard faculty and later headed the graduate school. Miss Elsie was not just a talented, diligent piano student, she befriended world-class musicians, especially world-class pianists. She used her relationships to impact others positively.

Juilliard's graduate music program was first offered in 1924, and it was only available to students on a scholarship study basis. It was an exclusive program—very difficult to get into. Bomar Cramer (1900-1974, pupil of both Josef and Rosina Lhevinne for six years and the first recipient of a graduate fellowship in piano at Juilliard) no doubt encountered the indomitable, effervescent Elsie Sweeney when she visited New York City. Cramer had presented a successful town-hall recital at Aeolian Hall in New York which established his career nationally. Upon completing his graduate studies at Juilliard, he returned to Indianapolis, to head the piano department at Arthur Jordan Conservatory of Music. Piano, musical, and educational camaraderie among Elsie Sweeney, Wayne Berry, and Bomar Cramer was amazing.

Wayne Berry studied piano with Bomar Cramer and graduated from Arthur Jordan Conservatory of Music in 1932. Cramer coached him for his Juilliard audition. Wayne's exceptional talent was undeniable, but Elsie Sweeney's behind-the-scenes connections were "one-of-a-kind" remarkable; she helped all the musical pieces fit together. It is noteworthy that the 1929 stock market crash and ensuing economic depression did not alter Berry's plans; perhaps Elsie Sweeney played a key role in financial support.

Wayne Berry's Juilliard audition could make an engaging television episode. Bomar Cramer drew a map of Manhattan on the back of Berry's copy of Chopin *Nocturnes*. (Berry bequeathed to Beth Mays, one of his graduate students in piano at the Cincinnati Bible Seminary, the copy of the Nocturnes with the Manhattan map scrawled on the back.) More than fifty years later, Beth still had the handwritten map located in stacks of music Berry gave to her at his retirement from CBS in 1974–a touching remembrance. Below is Berry's audition account in his own words.[9]

> *"On the day of the audition, I was waiting on the second floor with other candidates. When my name was called, I was so nervous I could not speak. Inside the large audition room there were two Steinway concert grands and a long circular table, around which the following examiners were seated: Albert Spaulding, noted violinist; Josef Lhevinne and Rosina Lhevinne (Joseph had taught Elsie Sweeney in Berlin, and both had taught Bomar Cramer); Olga Samaroff, wife of Leopold Stokowski (conductor of the*

Philadelphia Symphony Orchestra); Albert Stoessel, violinist and conductor of the New York Oratorical Society; Georges Berrier, renowned flutist; and Ernest Hutcheson, noted Australian pianist and director of Juilliard.

"Hutcheson asked me to play Beethoven's Pathetique Sonata. After playing about half of the first movement, Hutcheson stopped me with these words, 'That's enough!' I played some of the required Chopin and Debussy selections, with the same result for each, and then I was dismissed without comment.

"Feeling completely discouraged and disillusioned, I packed my things and took the next train back to Indianapolis. When I arrived back in Columbus, there was a telegram announcing the winning fellowship and also the time of my first piano lesson ... with Ernest Hutcheson."[10]

Those of us who have sacrificed and "poured our souls" into preparing an audition know exactly what this situation would have felt like for E. Wayne Berry.

Noteworthy People and Details

Let's pause briefly to emphasize some background and details. From New York City to Columbus, Indiana, is more than seven hundred miles— that's a long train ride for Berry to spend dwelling on all he believed had gone wrong during his audition ... what should he have done ... and what would he do next? He had put everything on the line in front of world-class experts.

The faculty who heard Berry's audition were the crème-de-la-creme of the classical musical world at that moment. Wars and persecutions in Europe during the twentieth century forced outstanding musicians to flee to the United States where a large, first-class group of artists not only performed, but became conductors, composers, and teachers at leading conservatories and universities. Juilliard was at the very top of this group of schools, many of which traced their histories back almost a century to the time East-Coast money—and some snobbery—were developing. Columbus had sent its favorite son to Juilliard, and he was accepted.

Berry's piano teacher, Ernest Hutcheson (1871-1951), was a virtuoso sensation of his time. He had been a child prodigy, touring his native Australia at age five. His career had taken him to London, Leipzig, and Berlin, and he distinguished himself as a solo performer, even presenting three piano concertos (Tchaikovsky, Liszt, and MacDowell) in one performance—an incredible feat which he repeated once more in his career—only his second performance feat included three Beethoven concertos. Hutcheson was a strong proponent of radio broadcasts for music education.

He was also associated with the New York Chautauqua, where he provided respite for his good friend, George Gershwin, to complete Piano Concerto in F. Gershwin was already famous for his popular music, especially *Rhapsody in Blue*, but he struggled to get away from his adoring public in order to concentrate, compose, and meet stringent demands of Walter Damrosch (1862-1950), conductor of the New York Symphony Orchestra. Hutcheson was another one of Elsie Sweeney's piano teachers during some of her New York musical enrichment trips, and some of his compositions remain in her music cabinet at the Inn at Irwin Gardens—the former Irwin-Sweeney-Miller mansion.

Berry rubbed shoulders with the great and near great of every musical genre in the "Big Apple." He cited his experiences in New York and at Juilliard as very enriching. He was challenged and stimulated by ambitious students, the great organ at nearby Riverside Church (built by John D. Rockefeller and completed in 1930), and all the concerts. He was like a sponge, soaking up all the musical offerings, to the point Ernest Hutcheson finally advised him to limit himself to "about four concerts each week." Such a concert diet still provided quite a regular musical banquet. [11]

Throughout his Juilliard education, while Elsie campaigned for Wayne's career as "the next Bomar Cramer," pressure from Nettie (Elsie's older sister), was constantly applied for Berry to enter the field of religious music and return to Columbus. This pressure, along with hearing great music in New York churches and experiencing worship enriched by such music, all helped Wayne to eventually decide to concentrate on church music.[12] One can imagine Elsie and Nettie using all the influencing skills they could muster to maintain their loving, yet powerful tug-of-war for the future of Berry's outstanding musical gifts. There were so many compelling, interesting personalities and events.

Return to Columbus and Tabernacle Church

Berry returned to Columbus and on May 12, 1934, married his sweetheart from school days, Frances Pearce. He had accompanied her in various performances since high school; and the two were also together at church, since she was a member at Tabernacle. Pearce was a coloratura soprano and became known as an oratorio soloist and recitalist. Her first voice teacher was Ida Edinburn, who was one of Wayne's teachers in high school. Pearce studied in Indianapolis and later with Dan Beddoe (1863-1937), renowned Welsh tenor and oratorio soloist, at the College-Conservatory of Music in Cincinnati. She remained the leading soprano soloist at the Christian church and in Columbus until the Berrys left town in 1966. She also taught voice at the Cincinnati Bible Seminary for a few years.

Upon Wayne Berry's return to Tabernacle Church of Christ as organist, he went to Franklin College, Franklin, Indiana (about twenty miles north of Columbus), and persuaded the president, Dr. William Gear Spenser (1886-1960), to allow him to develop an instrumental program for the college.[14] In addition to teaching responsibilities at Franklin, Berry continued to spend one day each week at Butler University's College of Religion as special lecturer in church music. (W. G. Irwin and Hugh Th. Miller used their influence for Berry to teach at Butler, where he did so for more than twenty years.)

Soon, Wayne and Frances spent the summer of 1935 studying at Northfield, Massachusetts, with John Finley Williamson (1887-1964), president of Westminster Choir Summer School. This was a fortuitous encounter for two reasons. First, the immersive experience with a cappella singing and intense work in conducting provided a great impetus for Berry's own choral conducting, and after this summer, Nettie urged him to form the Columbus A Cappella Choir. His involvement in sacred choral music never waned during the remainder of his career. Second, this summer opportunity helped to cement a relationship between Berry and Williamson, who, a few years later, facilitated an expedited schedule for him to complete a master's degree at Westminster in a shorter time frame.

E. Wayne Berry was a hometown Columbus talent, reared and educated in Indiana, and groomed at world-renown musical institutions. Local Columbus influence prepared him for New York, Princeton—and other places—to develop skills and rub shoulders with world-class musicians. A family's wealth and influence brought him back home and paved the way for his influence in musical Columbus—and beyond. The Irwins, Sweeneys and Millers recognized and cultivated natural talent and inclination in hometown heroes; they exercised profound influence in finance, business, education, architecture, and Christian endeavors. Their wealth and influence were obvious in the investment they made in E. Wayne Berry's musical career and his outpouring of music to the community and Indiana for over four decades.

1. Personal letter from E. Wayne Berry, August 27, 1988, p. 1.
2. Ibid.
3. Ibid., p. 2.
4. *The Evening Republican*, May 28, 1927.

5. Letter from Berry, p. 3.
6. Ibid., p. 4.
7. Ibid.
8. Ibid., p. 5.
9. Employment Agreement between E. Wayne Berry and Tabernacle Church of Christ, March 3, 1929.
10. "Bomar Cramer Pleases," timesmachine.nytimes.com. Thursday, October 14, 1926, p. 22.
11. Letter from Berry, p. 6.
12. Ibid.
13. Ibid.
14. Ibid.
15. Ibid., p. 8.
16. Ibid.
17. *The Evening Republican*, August 1, 1936.

Chapter Six: Berry Comes of Age

One might mark E. Wayne Berry's return to Columbus from Juilliard as the moment when never-ending musical projects began to pour forth. It was a new reference point. Notwithstanding his study at Juilliard, summer at Westminster, establishment of the Columbus A Cappella Choir, and employment as full-time organist-choir director at Tabernacle Church of Christ—all significant milestones—these events were not ends in themselves. They simply paved the way for musical fulfillment to come.

Onward to Quite a Career

I cite two other significant milestones. The first occurred when Nettie Miller, once again, sent Wayne and Frances on another choral enrichment sojourn—this time to Ephraem, Wisconsin, to study with father and son, F. Melius and Olaf Christiansen, conductors of the world-renowned St. Olaf Choir. It was probably the summer of 1937. The St. Olaf Choir has existed for over a century, maintaining a tradition of choral excellence firmly established since 1912. Numerous recordings and YouTube videos still attest to the choir's artistry today. Nettie paid for both Berrys to attend a summer of study with the famed Christiansens; I think she knew how much Frances was a part of Wayne's ministry at Tabernacle.

It is important to recall, besides church programming, teaching at Franklin College, Butler University, and the press toward a new sanctuary and organ, a second milestone needed to be achieved before Wayne's musical efforts could be defined and focused primarily on Columbus. He needed the credibility a master's degree from Westminster Choir College would provide. John Finley Williamson (1887-1964) had established his distinctive choir in 1920 at Westminster Presbyterian Church in Dayton, Ohio. Then, in 1926 he founded the school associated with the choir, and his Westminster Choir College later moved to Princeton, New Jersey, in 1932 for its permanent home. Williamson was impressed with Berry since working with him in the summer of 1935, to the point of designing an academic program for him to complete his master's degree in one year, rather than two—all to keep him in Columbus as much as possible.

Westminster also provided Berry crucial association with organist Carl Weinrich (1904-1991), a relationship which would result in a huge win for Columbus in the not-too-distant future. Weinrich was famous and well-qualified, having attended New York University and the Curtis Institute of Music. He studied organ with Lynnwood Farnum (Canadian organist who became the preeminent organist in 1920s North America) and French organist, Marcel Dupré.

Weinrich was an outstanding organist and teacher who served on the faculty of several leading schools: Princeton (where he was director of music at University Chapel), Wellesley, Columbia, Vassar, and, of course, Westminster. He was a recitalist who toured extensively and was known for his recordings of J. S. Bach's organ works. During the 1930s, he was a leader for the Baroque music revival in the USA; however, he did not scorn contemporary organ music. Weinrich programmed many contemporary works into his recitals.

Berry summed up the influence of his Westminster master's study as follows:

> *"The college work was great; all of it was directed toward what I wished to accomplish in Columbus. The organ program was intense. Everything had to be as nearly perfect as possible—Mr. Weinrich played that way! (He also played tennis the same way!) The entire college student body formed a choir, and we sang with the New York Philharmonic Orchestra. One performance which made a lasting impression on me was singing the Bach B Minor Mass in Princeton Chapel. All of this added up to a marvelous learning experience, a fine preparation for later work."*[1]

__Author's Reflection:__ There are two insights from Berry's summary of his master's work at Westminster which caught my attention. The reference to tennis indicates Berry and Weinrich (only five years older) played together; it appears tennis helped to seal a friendship between them. (Indeed, Berry and J. Irwin Miller had been avid tennis players, too.) The newspaper account from August 1, 1936, tells us Wayne must have been very competitive. The Evening Republican states that although Berry was favored to win a tennis tournament, he lost.[2] Obviously he had played and won often enough to warrant a winning reputation for people to follow.

The second insight from the summary is that E. Wayne Berry sang in choir at Westminster.[3] Those of us who studied with him at CBS never heard him sing. E. Wayne Berry's choirs were always known for their precision and clear articulation. In my personal experience at the Cincinnati Bible Seminary, I never remember hearing Berry sing, demonstrate tone production, or vowel formation/color to his choir. He told us what he wanted, but never sang. However, his reference to "singing the Bach B Minor Mass" and singing "with the New York Philharmonic" indicate he did sing during his Westminster study.

Berry shared insights into choral singing he witnessed and learned at Westminster. There were always so many singers with perfect pitch that no one ever played a chord or blew a pitch pipe before the choir started to sing; pitch was ever-so-quietly hummed among the choir, and the first chord was sung basically "out-of-the-blue." Impressive. The Westminster Choir was one of the first choirs to communicate effectively, accompanied by a large professional orchestra, such as the New York Philharmonic.

Berry also said there were strict rules about women's hair and makeup. The choir's visual appearance on stage was to be uniform—a vital aspect of effective communication, even before singing commenced. Choir members had daily assigned physical exercises, too, to keep them in the best physical shape for singing; I believe they even had to include some running.

There were other choral lessons gleaned from Berry's Westminster experiences. He emphasized that an excellent choir can be built with average voices—excellent choral sound is not dependent upon solo quality. Solo voices do not necessarily equate to excellent choral tone. He believed maximum choral volume can be produced from thirty to thirty-five voices; simply adding more voices did not create more sound, unless more sopranos were added—more soprano sound added to the overall choral volume. I also learned that you can usually balance one-third men's voices to two-thirds women's voices. Berry's choral insights served me well throughout my career, however, I DID sing, demonstrating desired tone and vowels to all my choirs.

Nettie Miller's ability to envision a musical future for Wayne Berry, her community, and church is remarkable. Of course, she had great financial resources at her disposal, but her influence progressed beyond her wealth. It was as if she could look back—but see the future, and thus, develop an effective strategy to move forward and accomplish her vision. The concept of modern architecture for Tabernacle's new church was presented by her son, J. Irwin, and she got on board completely. She laid out her vision for an exceptional organ and passed it to Wayne Berry for fulfillment. Her concept of the function and power of excellent choral music provided the impetus for what she challenged Berry to develop through the A Cappella Choir. Her ideas became reality in amazing fashion. Providing possibilities and funding for Wayne Berry's choral skills was part of her musical legacy. Furthermore, she helped him connect with key musicians who were in the prime of life, career, and influence—all with the goal of positive impact in Columbus, Indiana.

Berry's A Cappella Choir was launched in 1935, and the ensemble programmed independently until after he assumed leadership of the church choir from Claude Smith. (He became full-time at church in 1938 and started conducting the church choir.) The A Cappella Choir membership was eventually absorbed into the regular church choir. However, *The Evening Republican* referenced a new season for the elite ensemble beginning in April 1940.[4]

It reported the church was full (over 900 attended in the old Tabernacle, in spite of rain), and an appreciative audience representing almost every church in the city attended. The choral program included chorales, contemporary works, and a couple of negro spirituals. It appears that the choir had strong grass-roots fame and following from the local community. This is an amazing reality for a Midwestern town in the early years of World War II.

Students of twentieth-century choral music must give attention to the contributions of F. Melius Christiansen (1871-1955), his son, Olaf (1901-1984), and the work of John Finley Williamson (1887-1964). Not only were these men effective pioneers, their contributions are still valued today. They were cutting-edge experts in choral music. Extensive research into their philosophy, methods, repertoire, and distinctive choral sound still exists to benefit today's choirs.

Throughout my study, career, and research, I have found it rewarding to note how much of their choral knowledge and technique was passed along to me through Professor Berry. Amazingly, E. Wayne Berry studied under all three choral authorities during time he spent with the St. Olaf and Westminster choirs. Columbus singers were recipients of Berry's wonderful choral associations—all brought home to the Hoosier heartland. Furthermore, *all* of Berry's singers at CBS received these blessings—even if they never realized their origin. But … Nettie imagined it all.

1. Letter from Berry, p. 9.
2. *The Evening Republican*, August 1, 1936.
3. Information from classes, lectures, informal conversations with E. Wayne Berry through years of association.
4. *The Evening Republican*, 1940.

Chapter Seven: Joe and Ed

It seems everyone knows a Joe and Ed. Every type of community—church, school, team—has some version of the twosome. They are about the same age, have similar interests, and hang out together. In Columbus, Indiana, Joe and Ed were born less than five months apart. Both were involved at Tabernacle Church of Christ; both played tennis and loved music—especially the music of J. S. Bach. Now this last fact separates other friends from Joe's and Ed's relationship. This is where the commonality of my Joe and Ed analogy breaks down, because these young men were anything but usual with their musical tastes, interests, and life pursuits. I move ahead and call them by their full names—Joseph and Edgar—but, not for long.

Joseph and Edgar were uniquely musical soulmates. They made music together at Joseph's home, at church, in the community, and throughout the state. As they matured, both thought deeply about the music they pursued: Edgar pursued his music as vocation; Joseph pursued his music as avocation. Edgar played piano and organ and conducted choirs; Joseph played violin and sang tenor in Edgar's choirs. Both were influenced greatly by Joseph's family members. Both Edgar and Joseph enjoyed outstanding educational opportunities because of Joseph's generous, classy family, especially his mother and his aunt. Both had mutual good friends in the creative genius Clessie and gifted attorney Edwin. Edgar and Joseph married hometown girls and had daughters born in 1943.

Both Edgar and Joseph returned home following impressive formal education at world class institutions and built careers in Columbus. Both Edgar and Joseph were men of deep personal convictions, even though theese convictions eventually led them to part ways. Joseph and Edgar both died in 2004; Joseph was ninety-five—Edgar, just six months shy of his ninety-fifth birthday. They were commonly known throughout their adult lives by a first initial, full middle name, and, of course, a last name. In case you haven't figured it out by now, Ed—Edgar—was E. Wayne Berry and Joe—Joseph—was J. Irwin Miller. Both were incredibly influential in their fields and demonstrated integrity in their pursuits.

Here are details to fill in the summary above and complete the story below:

- J. Irwin Miller May 26, 1909-August 16, 2004
- E. Wayne Berry October 13, 1909-March 16, 2004

Author's Note: *I did not make the ironic connections of E. Wayne Berry and J. Irwin Miller, nor understand the depth of their significance, until very recently in compiling my research. Professor Berry had indicated in a letter to me that he and J. Irwin were about the same age, good friends, and grew up together. He said they remained friends until he left Columbus to teach at CBS. That was all he said. As I found more printed programs, newspaper articles, read Charles Rentschler's 2014 biography of J. Irwin Miller, and started to align facts, it fell in place that the two men had shared deeply in the ups and downs of life, while making so much music together. Furthermore, I personally believe J. Irwin's split from First Christian Church in the mid-1950s was the death-blow to their uniquely close musical relationship. I think Berry wanted to avoid rekindling old wounds by simply summarizing for me the past relationship with Miller, not recalling details.*

Family Music

Elsie Sweeney (J. Irwin's aunt) took a special interest in both J. Irwin and E. Wayne. She strategized for Wayne's career as concert pianist—in her mind. Her European studies and New York City musical sojourns provided great wealth to share with budding musicians and these two young men. Visions of Juilliard began to dance in her head for young Wayne, especially as he became organist at age fifteen for a congregation of a thousand people. Meanwhile, Elsie and her sister Nettie had taught violin to Clementine and her younger brother, J. Irwin, as they were growing up.

The sisters could enjoy ensembles, especially when Clementine (whose first goal was to become a concert violinist) transitioned to cello. Wayne remembered the three of them playing easier piano trios from classical literature, however they never performed publicly. He even composed a trio for piano, violin, and cello,[1] which they practiced and performed in the music room where three generations of Irwins, Sweeneys, and Millers found musical delight.

The mansion, directly across the street from church, provided fertile soil where many musical, artistic, and architectural ideas—business ventures, too—took root and grew to full-flower during the first half of the twentieth century. It really was a modern-day version of the Renaissance Florentine Camerata in Columbus, Indiana. Quite amazing creations and interactions took place in the mansion housing three generations.

Both Return to Columbus

Wayne Berry returned to Columbus from advanced study at Juilliard in 1933. He continued as organist at Tabernacle, started an instrumental program at Franklin College, and spent one day a week a Butler University's college of Religion as special lecturer in church music (thanks to the influence of W. G. Irwin and Hugh Th. Miller). In 1934, he married Frances Pearce. He was industrious and so was J. Irwin Miller, who graduated from Yale in 1931, where he studied Greek and Latin, graduating Phi Beta Kappa and Magna Cum Laude. He continued graduate study at Oxford and completed a master's degree.

While studying at Oxford, Irwin played violin in the symphony, was a member of the rowing team, and took a European tour with W.G., or "Unk."[2] He, too, returned to Columbus in 1933 and took a position at Cummins Engine Company in 1934. His amazing business career was launched. Both E. Wayne and J. Irwin returned home with first-class educations, outstanding experiences, and excellent prospects—Wayne's music was all-consuming; J. Irwin kept up with his music, too, in the midst of burgeoning business pursuits.

E. Wayne and J. Irwin in Joint Musical Performances

For Christmas, 1934, it seems everyone was back home, making holiday music together at Tabernacle. Claude "Smitty" Smith conducted a cantata, *The Story of Christmas* by Alexander Matthews. Wayne Berry was the organist; G. Chester Kitzinger and J. Irwin Miller assisted on violin.[3] Soloists were Frances Berry, soprano; Dorothy Poulton, contralto (see chapter fourteen); Walter Norman, John and Jeffrey VanNorman, tenors; Gerald Haislup, baritone; Olvey Lewellen, bass. Children's choirs participated under the direction of Mrs. Ray Weed for the girls and Charles Sewell for the boys.

__Author's thought:__ J. Irwin Miller and G. Chester Kitzinger were the violinists, and both were exceptional players. Kitzinger was a conservatory-trained professional. It is likely he became J. Irwin's violin teacher when he progressed to more advanced violin study beyond what mother Nettie and Aunt Elsie taught at home.

It was the height of the Great Depression, but Nettie Miller's focus was elsewhere. In 1935, she funded a rewarding summer for Wayne and Frances to study choral music with John Finley Williamson of Westminster's

Choir Summer School in Northfield, Massachusetts.[4] Upon their return home, Nettie initiated what turned out to be a life-changing project for Wayne. She suggested that he start a select choir to perform a cappella music and hone his conducting skills.[5]

Nettie had her eyes set on the future—urging Wayne to focus on sacred music and serve the Tabernacle congregation full time—as soon as possible. (Her vision for Wayne was taking the lead over Elsie's vision.) The response to Nettie's idea of an a cappella choir resulted in an excellent musical ensemble of near-professional quality. Projects were lining up for success in the Irwin-Sweeney-Miller world of innovation, business leadership, and music leadership for church and community. Twenty-five-year-old friends, J. Irwin and E. Wayne were ready to assume their roles. Although E. Wayne was the key figure for immediate musical success, J. Irwin's participation grew ever more crucial in musical aspects soon to transpire.

The Columbus A Cappella Choir

Clementine, J. Irwin, and E. Wayne now made choral music together, moving beyond the piano/string trios they played years earlier in the family's music room. The Columbus A Cappella Choir became a reality through the vision of Nettie Miller, Clementine and J. Irwin's mother. As it evolved, it provided choral music on a new level in Columbus. Berry invited eighteen members from the church to form a choir, and they practiced a cappella music intensely, simply for the fun of it.

At the same time, the ensemble provided Wayne a choir with which to practice his conducting. Clementine (alto) and J. Irwin (tenor) sang in Wayne's choir, which soon caught the thrill of singing together and were willing to practice long hours to accomplish a quality of singing not yet heard in Columbus.[6] The ensemble practiced many months without considering a concert; but the A Cappella Choir began to give concerts in Columbus and throughout the state. They achieved an outstanding reputation in Indiana.

Berry was able to expand his choral conducting technique with another summer of study—this time in Ephraem, Wisconsin, with Dr. F. Melius Christiansen, and his son, Olaf Christiansen, esteemed conductors of the internationally famous St. Olaf Choir. That choir's sound had greatly influenced the Westminster Choir sound in its early years.[7] Both choirs set the standard for modern choral singing as the twentieth century progressed. Again, Frances accompanied Wayne for this summer of intense, specialized choral study; again, Nettie Miller covered all expenses.

Reminiscent of Jennie Bates more than five decades earlier, choral music took on new emphasis and flourished at Tabernacle Church of Christ. A Cappella Choir members sang in, and provided excellent leadership for, the church choir, still led by Claude Smith, beloved director since 1921. Berry related an important fact for readers to consider: A Cappella Choir members were solo-ists and exceptional sight-readers;[8] his assessment indicates the high level of musicianship Clementine and J. Irwin possessed and provided for the choir.

Since the real purpose of the A Cappella Choir was to heighten and underline the religious intent of music sung in church, the concert emphasis of the en-semble eventually faded. Within a few years after Berry became director of the church choir in 1938, the select ensemble was absorbed into the regular church choir so members could put their full energy into the development and ongo-ing activities of that group. As technical aspects of choral singing improved, the choir became more concerned with the spiritual message of the music.[9]

Pause for a Look Back: Tying Threads Together

Joseph Ireland Irwin's love of music and dedication to song leading almost a century earlier had been carried on and transformed through Irwin family lead-ership and investment. His granddaughter Nettie, great-granddaughter Clemen-tine, and great-grandson J. Irwin built on his faithful example and love of sing-ing through their participation, forward-thinking, and all-around strategizing as members of the Columbus A Cappella Choir. Furthermore, in 1938, E. Wayne Berry became full-time organist and choir director for Tabernacle Church of Christ, fulfilling the dream Nettie Irwin Sweeney Miller had passionately pur-sued for him and undergirded with her generous financial support. Her family had bequeathed quite a musical legacy, and more was to come.

It is important to note that Claude C. Smith continued to sing in Taberna-cle's choir after Wayne Berry became director, thus smoothing leadership challenges which could have caused problems. Such a successful leader-ship transition speaks well for all who were involved. In numerous church-es this situation could have split the congregation.

Now, let us return our attention to the 1930s.

Big Plans for the Future

After J. Irwin Miller joined Cummins Engine Company in 1934, he pur-sued more innovations, working with uncle W. G. Irwin and inventor Cles-sie Cummins. He was very close to both remarkable men, but sometimes found himself in the middle of back-and-forth disagreements between the company's co-founders. By navigating such issues, J. Irwin acquired skills and perspectives which would serve him well for the rest of his life in business administration.

During studies at Yale, Irwin took an architectural appreciation course, and it captured his imagination. Simply put, when family discussions at the mansion turned toward construction of a new building for Tabernacle, plans progressed quickly and seriously. The family, especially Nettie, eventually got on-board with the innovative, modern architectural style J. Irwin advocated. His influence in architecture grew rapidly, and architecture became an incredibly important emphasis for the entire city of Columbus. In time, J. Irwin Miller charted a vision which positioned Columbus on the national—indeed international stage—for modern architecture.

On Sunday, May 31, 1936, J. Irwin Miller's grandmother, Linnie Irwin Sweeney, and Linnie's brother, W. G. Irwin, presented an entire city block as a gift to the church (cater-cornered across Fifth Street from the family mansion) for constructing a new building.[10] This gift was reminiscent of their ancestor, Benjamin Irwin, who gave a corner of his farm for the congregation's first log church building in 1824. (Benjamin Irwin was W. G. and Linnie's great uncle.) W. G. chaired the committee for the new building, and J. Irwin's mother, Nettie, was the only woman to serve on it.

Nettie functioned as musical advocate for the new facility—its pipe organ, acoustics, choral suite, and all details such aspects demanded. She involved Wayne Berry closely in planning, even as he was developing the exceptional choral program she had envisioned for the church. Despite the Great Depression, everyone was very focused on a bright future in Columbus. Although the world was also careening to war, there was no stopping the Irwin-Sweeney-Miller family as they steered, full-steam ahead with dreams for their church.

In 1938, Wayne Berry was granted a year's leave of absence from Tabernacle and Franklin College to pursue a Master of Sacred Music degree at Westminster Choir College, Princeton, New Jersey. Because of his 1935 summer choral studies, he was well-known to the school through John Finley Williamson. The faculty arranged a special schedule for him to complete his master's work in one year, instead of two.[11] Furthermore, he began to study organ with Bach expert Carl Weinrich (1904-1991). Berry and Weinrich, who was only five years older, struck up a close friendship, which was also cemented on the tennis court.

Weinrich became an adjunct player, so-to-speak, in the Irwin-Swee-ney-Miller family project for Tabernacle's new church organ. The planning team now included not only the entire philanthropic family, but also world-famous architects Eliel Saarinen and his son Eero Saarinen, plus noted scholar, conductor, and organist Carl Weinrich. Both E. Wayne Berry and J. Irwin Miller, though still in their late twenties, functioned as key players for the forward-thinking team's projects for Tabernacle Church of Christ.

Very Memorable Concerts

J. Irwin and Clementine continued to sing in the church choir. By 1940, Tabernacle's choir (now led by E. Wayne Berry) was well-known throughout Indiana and participated in impressive musical presentations with Indiana University. On December 8, 1940, at the university, the church choir joined I.U.'s choral union, symphony, and men's and women's glee clubs to perform Bach's *Christmas Oratorio*, Vaughan Williams' *Fantasia on Christmas Carols*, and portions of Handel's *Messiah*. Robert L. Sanders, dean of the School of Music, conducted.[12] This extraordinary program was definitely outside the norm for a church choir, but Tabernacle's choir was exceptional.

Another memorable program occurred on May 4, 1941, when the church choir appeared in a benefit concert for the Indianapolis Symphony Orchestra at Indiana University Auditorium. The choir performed Bach's Cantata No. 106, *Gottes Zeit ist die allerbeste Zeit* (God's Time is Best), accompanied by the Indiana University Symphony Orchestra. Robert Sanders conducted the performance in which members of the Indianapolis Symphony Orchestra were special guests in the audience.[13] How unusual it was that a church choir helped to raise funds for a symphony orchestra, but E. Wayne Berry's choir was equal to the opportunity and challenge; Clementine and J. Irwin contributed their musical talent in performances, as well as financial support as donors for the symphony.

Elsie Sweeney was a chief influencer in this combined fund-raising effort. The printed program for May 4, 1941, lists E. Wayne Berry; Herman Berg, head of the violin department at Depauw University; and Ruggero Vené, guest conductor of Indiana University's concert choir. The program included a message of support from Gov. Henry F. Schricker. All living members of the Irwin-Sweeney-Miller family (W. G. Irwin, Linnie Irwin Sweeney, Elsie Sweeney, Nettie Sweeney Miller, Hugh Th. Miller, Clementine Miller and J. Irwin Miller) were listed as patrons or donors.[14] The printed program also indicates that Robert Stone Tangeman, professor of music at I.U., contributed all program notes; Tangeman later became husband to Clementine Miller and professor at The Union Theological Seminary School of Sacred Music.

On December 7, 1941, Tabernacle's choir again joined Indiana University's choral union and symphony to repeat essentially the same program combined groups had presented a year earlier. Sanders conducted the concert, which was given as part of dedication ceremonies for the new School of Music Auditorium. This was a noteworthy event for another reason. Upon leaving the auditorium after the concert, choir members were stunned to read newspaper extras announcing the bombing of Pearl Harbor.[15]

__Author's Note:__ At age thirty-two, Robert L. Sanders (1906-1974) became the youngest dean of the school of music at Indiana University—a record which still stands today. He had no administrative experience, but was a highly respected performer, organist, and conductor commended for his social skills. Sanders was a very energetic promoter of music at I.U., and, no doubt, worked well with Wayne Berry, especially through the efforts and influence of Elsie Sweeney. Berry and Sanders were at similar career points in building music programs with fine reputations for their respective institutions. Nettie's choral vision for E. Wayne and the church had been realized.

Many Hurdles in the 1940s

War was only one of a series of events during the 1940s which altered J. Irwin Miller's musical and business plans. The 1940s also came with great challenges for Wayne Berry. However, for a few moments, both men—now in their early thirties—could pause to celebrate their successes as Tabernacle moved into its landmark new structure housing the magnificent organ. Both J. Irwin and E. Wayne had given whole-heartedly of their time and influence to the project. The building was dedicated debt-free at a cost of about $750,000. (over $14 million in today's dollars).

Ten special morning and evening dedication services were presented in the new church on Sundays beginning May 31, 1942, and concluding on the evening of June 28, 1942; two services were concerts. On Sunday evening, June 21, E. Wayne Berry played a dedicatory recital on the new Aeolian-Skinner organ; and, on Sunday evening, June 28, the choir presented Mendelssohn's *Hymn of Praise* to conclude dedication festivities. Later in 1942 Tabernacle Church of Christ formally changed its name to The Christian Church.[16] From 1955 on, the congregation has been known as First Christian Church.

The congregation charted a bold, innovative course with its new building, and national notice quickly ensued. Some townspeople and curious visitors were slow to appreciate the new architecture which stood out in stark contrast to surrounding buildings. Inside the sanctuary, very live acoustics heightened the brilliance of an organ sound which was also new to Midwesterners. Therefore, plenty of criticism was voiced. J. Irwin and E. Wayne would not have been immune or unaware of the criticism, since they were key figures in the architecture and organ design, but they were young and resilient.

J. Irwin joined the US Navy and graduated from basic training as a lieutenant on August 8, 1942, second in his class of 750.[17] He had been dating Xenia Simons before leaving Columbus, and in a surprise to his family, married her on February 5, 1943, in Washington, D.C. No family members attended, but Clessie Cummins was best man. W. G. came for a brief visit before J. Irwin boarded his ship. It would turn out to be the last time W. G. and nephew would ever see each other. W. G. died while J. Irwin was at sea.

Back in Columbus, Wayne Berry became father to a second daughter in 1943. J. Irwin, too, became a father of a daughter in December 1943; Xenia gave birth while he served on the aircraft carrier *Langley* in the Pacific. Although growing families delighted both fathers, layers of responsibility and life-changing events were soon to complicate the lives of both men.

War and Deaths Change Plans

W. G. Irwin's sudden death in late 1943 left a huge void at Cummins Engine Company with the passing of one of its founders. Everyone was in shock. The company had vital war contracts with the United States government, so J. Irwin applied for a discharge from the Navy to return home and manage the business. However, it took a second, later request following the death of his grandmother, Linnie (less than two months later), on February 2, 1944, for him to be discharged.

Back in Columbus, he needed to sort out serious issues in the family business—a business, at long-last profitable and employing some 1,800 workers, yet facing crucial junctures.[18] Meanwhile, Clementine Irwin Miller served her country by joining the Red Cross; she was stationed in Italy, near the front lines, in 1944.[19] Thus, until J. Irwin returned from the Pacific, only Nettie, Hugh Th., and Elsie were left in Columbus to maintain Irwin-Sweeney-Miller interests in all family owned businesses, let alone all other involvements at church and in the community.

These huge changes in family dynamics meant there was scaled-back leadership for all family projects. However, scaled-back leadership was only in place a few years when J. Irwin's father, Hugh Th. Miller, died on May 26, 1947. In less than four years, Irwin-Sweeney-Miller leadership changed dramatically, and so had J. Irwin's role.

Hugh Th. Miller had filled several key positions in the family's businesses and community endeavors. At Cummins, Clessie left the engine company in late 1944, though he didn't officially retire until 1951; J. Irwin had become executive vice president, and his father was chairman of the board.[20] Hugh Th. Miller had also been chairman of the board at First Christian Church, and president of Irwin Union Bank and Trust. He was highly respected as a trusted leader in all endeavors; together with Nettie, the couple made a great philanthropic husband/wife duo to head various worthy projects. Three significant family losses in less than four years compounded stress for J. Irwin and could have understandably overwhelmed him. Nevertheless, he rose to the occasion and lived up to the family's example of strength in every way.

Music Programs Grow

All the above changes took J. Irwin and Clementine out of the church's music ministry for a while, but Wayne Berry maintained a very active musical program. The building was new; the organ was new; and expectations were high. Berry played three different programs of congregational organ favorites during 1942. The 160-foot tower created new possibilities, too. For several years, beginning in 1944, children's, high school, and adult choirs broadcast preludes of choral music from the tower each Easter.[21] The Christian Church continued to have special musical presentations for Christmas, Easter, and various special occasions. The church also was involved in other musical activities with community-wide participation. The Apollo Boys' Choir of Dallas, Texas, presented a program on April 12, 1945.[22] The next month, on May 27, the Civic Choral Society, composed of choirs from First Methodist, First Presbyterian, First Christian, and the Baptist church, presented a concert of thanksgiving and patriotic music celebrating the end of World War II.[23] On December 16, the Civic Choral Society performed selections from the Christmas portion of *Messiah*. Both Civic Choral Society programs were presented at the Christian Church with E. Wayne Berry as accompanist.[24] The church also featured a new community choir, the Noblett-Sparks Men's Chorus, in concert on June 24, 1945.[25] J. W. Hartley, a member of First Christian Church, conducted this program.

It was a very busy time for all types of musical activities, and E. Wayne Berry administrated all of them. He, with members of the congregation, compiled two publications, *Christian Hymns* in 1945, and *Songs for Preschool Children* in 1946 (see chapter fourteen for Dorothy Poulton's involvement). The church took advantage of the availability of Columbus' new elementary music supervisor, Miss Betty Frantz, beginning in September 1946, when they hired her to relieve some of Wayne Berry's workload with children's and high school choirs.[26] Miss Frantz came to Columbus from Frankfort, Indiana.

Significant Organ Recital

A highlight for Wayne Berry was his organ recital sponsored by the American Guild of Organists on October 22, 1946.[27] This was an auspicious occasion for both Berry and the church. However, criticism of the organ volume and brilliant tone was expressed, and the guild wrote a critical appraisal. People were *not* accustomed to this sound, and the problem was partially addressed by re-voicing some of the pipes. Some of the negative press came because the organ sound was simply new to the ears of many guild attendees, even though they were trained organists.

Eventually, everyone settled down, and Berry was not permanently scarred by the negativity—he was confident in the knowledge and musicality of two international notables in the field, G. Donald Harrison and Carl Weinrich, who shared his perspective in creating the instrument. Generally, pipe organ sound innovation and expectation caught up to the cutting-edge developments demonstrated in Columbus. However, in the short term, the criticism hurt. Innovation has its price.

When one considers Berry's responsibilities (including his teaching at Franklin College and Butler University) in combination with the demands of a dynamic church and music program, not to mention a wife and two young daughters, it's no wonder he was stressed. Musicians understand how this kind of pressure eats away over time—even though they are doing what they love. Berry was doing what he loved, but he was also charting new territory and branching out, using instrumental resources from Indiana University School of Music to accompany programs at the church. There was a lot of reputation-building and maintaining on the line, particularly with the new building and organ. Berry was not yet forty years old.

Stress Relief and Diversion?

Perhaps to provide diversion and activity outside the intense realm of music, Wayne and Frances Berry purchased Fruitland Orchards in 1943.[28]

The orchard included 200 acres of apple and plum trees—approximately 5,000 trees in all—what a labor-intensive diversion. The Berrys lived outside Columbus with their two young daughters and operated the orchard for ten years. Wayne's love for growing fruit and the pressures of his musical responsibilities led him to resign his position at First Christian by the summer of 1947.[29] He also purchased an orange grove in Florida and spent part of his time there, although he and Frances still remained active with the church's music program whenever they were in Columbus. For a little over a year—until the fall of 1948–Berry did not serve in a paid position at church. In actuality, it was as if he was on sabbatical.

J. Irwin seemed to understand Wayne Berry's "burnout." He, himself, had experienced a monumental shift in workload when he returned to Columbus from World War II. And deaths of family members certainly compounded his situation and impacted his growing family. Furthermore, he suffered a case of polio in 1949 which left him with a life-long limp and unable to play tennis. But J. Irwin did not cast music aside because of increasing demands. He took the lead as spokesman for First Christian's music committee in presenting a budget for the church's 1947-48 program. More importantly, he included a detailed account of all aspects and demands of leading such a program. The resulting document was recorded in board minutes and provides invaluable insight into philosophical and practical musical matters. It is included in this book as chapter seventeen.

Irwin conferred with Wayne to compile his appraisal (also given to Wayne's replacement, Harold Frantz). No animosity was expressed, however he thoroughly voiced necessary concerns, and established his expertise as the Irwin-Sweeney-Miller's newest and very competent advocate for music.[30] Surely his mother was especially proud and thankful. One hundred years earlier, his great-grandfather Joseph Ireland Irwin (for whom he was named) had been leading music for the congregation—such an incredible connection. The preceding century had witnessed interwoven gifts from Irwins, Sweeneys, and Millers for church, community, and musical development in remarkable, quite amazing ways.

Things didn't work out for Wayne Berry in Florida, nor for Harold Frantz at First Christian Church. The result was Wayne Berry resumed his paid position at church in fall 1948.[31] There must have been significant improvement in the conditions and demands placed on Wayne, Frances, and their girls, because upon his return as full-time organist-choir director, he entered upon a period of renewed effectiveness and appeared to be rejuvenated in spirit. (Readers can see why I called Berry's time away a sabbatical.)

Piecing together a timeline—events, people, history, and resulting success—seems to indicate that positive ramifications grew (partially, at least) from the carefully-crafted philosophical/practical analysis written by J. Irwin Miller in 1947. His musical ancestors would have been gratified by his leadership and resulting detailed document. His analysis (chapter seventeen) is carefully worded, as one would expect from a CEO and business professional, describing the scope of music ministry. It represents the culmination of generations of musical emphasis passed on to him, and it includes the influence of his good musical friend since childhood, E. Wayne Berry. A certain amount of sadness must be recognized, too, as Miller and Berry's musical worlds were about to take divergent paths in the decade to follow.

Philosophy of Music

J. Irwin Miller's youngest son, Will, contributed valuable insights concerning his father's deeply held views on music, and those views have been recorded by Charles E. Mitchel Rentschler in his 2014 book, *The Cathedral Builder, A Biography of J. Irwin Miller*. I cite this profound conclusion, "music did not just supplement Miller's religiosity, it *suffused* his faith. Like reading the Bible, playing the violin was typically a daily occurrence."[32] Some may find it hard to believe, but Will Miller attests music was more important to his father than architecture.[33]

J. Irwin Miller required his five children to take piano lessons and practice every day.[34] This discipline certainly indicates Nettie's and Aunt Elsie's musical influence on Will's father.

Will Miller also recalled his father's instructions for his funeral. "The one thing I am adamant on is that my memorial service should include the music of J. S. Bach."[35] Irwin's love of Bach extended back decades, including the trios he, Clementine and Wayne played in the family's music room long ago. A printed program from July 2, 1953, indicates that J. Irwin played all four movements of J. S. Bach's Sonata in E Major, No. 3, BWV 1016, accompanied by E. Wayne Berry, for a garden party sponsored by the Women's Council of the church.[36] Following the church's centennial celebrations in 1952, this garden party performance was probably one of the last times E. Wayne and J. Irwin played music together.

In 1955, J. Irwin and about forty families left First Christian Church to establish what became North Christian Church. In 1964, the new church constructed a building designed by Eero Saarinen (Eliel's son) and Kevin Roche.[37] J. Irwin's friendship and admiration for Eero Saarinen's work prompted him to have Saarinen design and build his family home, known simply as Miller House. J. Irwin and Xenia had broken the family tradition of multi-generations living under one roof a few years before they constructed the 1952 Miller House.

Sadly, though Rentschler indicated that although J. Irwin played violin just about every day, he never played it at North Christian Church.[38] Wayne Berry and others attest to the fact[39] J. Irwin owned two incredibly valuable violins—a 1709 Stradivarius and a 1743 Guarneri—combined appraised value of $4 million–in 1991.[40] (That would be more than $9 million in today's dollars.)

Rentschler relates more insight into J. Irwin's violin playing:

> *"To maintain his technique, Miller practiced faithfully, often using Music Minus One, a long-playing orchestral recording less the solo part, which he supplied. And he took with him a violin often on business trips and always on vacation to Canada in summer and to Florida in winter."*[41]

When one considers all facets of this amazing executive, it is obvious he was as much musician as he was businessman, architectural innovator, man of faith, and social influencer. Music truly fed his soul and provided the heart for his many gifts.

E. Wayne Berry's and J. Irwin Miller's inter-woven musical lives provide us with exceptional, fascinating, and enigmatic connections. These men were born less than five months apart in 1909 and died exactly five months apart in 2004—amazing history with a strong musical component.

1. Letter from E. Wayne Berry, August 27, 1988, p. 4.
2. Rentschler, Charles E. Mitchell, *The Cathedral Builder: A Biography of J. Irwin Miller*, Bloomington, Indiana: AuthorHouse, 2014, p. 22.
3. *The Evening Republican*, December 20, 1934, p. 8.
4. Letter from Berry, p. 13.
5. Ibid.
6. Letter from Berry, p. 16.
7. Heather MacLaughlin. "F. Melius Christiansen and the St. Olaf Choir"
8. Letter from Berry, p. 16.
9. Ibid.
10. Ibid., p. 9.
11. Ibid.
12. Printed program.
13. Printed program
14. Survey of patron and donor lists on printed program.
15. Letter from Berry.
16. Dedication programs.
17. Ibid.
18. Rentschler
19. Ibid.
20. Rentschler, p. 39.

21. Rentschler, p. 46.
22. Letter from Berry
23. Ibid.
24. Ibid.
25. Ibid.
26. Ibid.
27. Ibid.
28. Ibid.
29. Letter from Berry, p. 16.
30. Ibid.
31. Ibid.
32. Ibid.
33. Rentschler, p. 53.
34. Ibid.
35. Ibid.
36. Rentschler, p. 153.
37. Printed program for the Garden Party.
38. Rentschler, p. 61.
39. Rentschler, p. 59.
40. Rentschler p. 53.
41. Ibid.
42. Ibid.

Chapter Eight: National Prominence

The 1940s may have been overflowing with professional and personal struggles in musical Columbus, but bigger obstacles and opportunities awaited in the 1950s. There were great victories ahead. There were soul-searching decisions ahead. There were inevitable challenges which had to be navigated. Wonderful memories were created as milestones were celebrated; difficult consequences had to be confronted to move forward. No one had it easy.

Edwin and Hazel Crouch

At Cummins Engine Company, J. Irwin Miller hired Edwin G. Crouch as chief legal counsel in 1939. Edwin was married to Hazel Payne Crouch, and the couple joined the Christian Church soon after their arrival. (They rented the first floor of Clessie Cummins' house for one year—more fascinating connections.) J. Irwin was always eager to have his key people at Cummins become members of the congregation which had been so close to his family for more than a century.

Edwin and Hazel were a natural fit, too. Hazel and her sister, Gladys, were nationally known song evangelists in Restoration Movement churches and were already well known at the Columbus church. They had used their musical talents at First Christian several times for special events in the past. Hazel was a fine gospel pianist and contralto; Gladys was more of a mezzo. The sisters always dressed alike, including fur stoles, which provided eye-catching accessories to their stylish, expensive outfits. You might say they fit-in by standing-out.

The Edwin Crouches immediately became active at church; Edwin served as an elder; Hazel sang in the choir, performed solos, played piano, and directed Vacation Bible School (she continued to do so for thirty-four years). Crouches, Berrys, and Millers were friends and very influential musically in the life of the community and church. They were leaders socially, as well as musically; the three husbands and their wives were highly respected; although Xenia Miller was not musical, she took a very active role in many other endeavors.

Author's Remembrance: *Growing up in the 1950s and 1960s, I had various opportunities to see and hear the Payne Sisters lead congregational* *singing and perform for very large Christian events, especially in Cincinnati, Ohio, downtown at Taft Auditorium. Wayne Berry played organ, and Hazel played piano. Hazel and Gladys usually included Frances Berry for vocal trios, accompanied by Wayne on piano. The Payne Sisters were born performers and very effective as leaders of congregational singing, but they were not above somewhat corny banter among themselves and Wayne Berry. People seemed to love it—they laughed and sang enthusiastically. Berry interacted with the "schticks" Hazel and Gladys initiated, always showing good humor and pleasant spirit. (However, his jaw constantly moved right and left ... hmm?) It was only during my college years that I learned Professor Berry was mortified by the antics of the Payne Sisters. He was a dignified, quiet man, who did not believe such shenanigans were appropriate—or necessary—for effective worship leading. But he went along, not participating any more than absolutely required by civility. I discovered his jaw movements were involuntary nervous demonstrations of discomfort and lack of approval.*

I also remember that Hazel, Gladys, and Frances' voices eventually displayed wide vibratos as they aged. My college friends rolled their eyes at the Payne Sisters and Frances Berry, and sadly, they became somewhat of a laughing stock to younger audiences, who did not appreciate such antics, voices, nor the fur stole trademarks people associated with performances. As I reflect, the 1950s and '60s were the end of an era for this type of gospel music leadership. Much later in life, I learned to appreciate what the Payne Sisters had contributed through their musical service—for their generation; however, I never modeled my leadership after their example.

Regular musical programming at the Christian Church upon E. Wayne Berry's return continued to grow. Mrs. Thelma Burnett was hired as assistant organist, and she was the only paid Berry assistant. Berry led the children's and high school choirs. Although these two choirs occasionally sang special numbers for services, they seldom gave complete programs by themselves. Each year at the closing program for Vacation Bible School, T. K. Smith (beloved preacher since 1930) presented awards to children's choir members with perfect attendance. By 1952 the children's choir involved about seventy, and the high school choir numbered about twenty-five.[1]

The adult choir maintained an active schedule. Besides regular programming at church, area choirs from First Christian Church in Bloomington, Franklin College, First Presbyterian Church, and First Methodist Church combined with the Christian Church in Columbus to present special concerts. Instrumentalists from Indiana University accompanied from time to time, as they had done since 1940. On April 28, 1950, the Christian

Church's choir sang a thirty-minute concert for the North American Christian Convention in Indianapolis.[2] Indiana University selected the choir to participate in the First Annual Invitational Church Choir Festival on May 4, 1951; only six choirs in the state received this honor.[3] Major choral works added to the choir's repertoire during the late 1940s and early 1950s included John Stainer's *Crucifixion* and *The Daughter of Jairus*, Mendelssohn's *St. Paul*, and Irene Berge's *The Cradle of Bethlehem*.[4]

Radio Broadcasts

Although television was still in its infancy, religious radio broadcasts became widespread in the early 1950s. The congregation's choir participated in many radio programs. Services and special concerts were heard on a local station, WCSI. At Christmas time in 1950, WLW radio, the "Nation's Station," in Cincinnati, chose the choir to perform Handel's *Messiah* for national broadcast. Instrumentalists from Indiana University assisted in the performances. The program was so well received that WLW repeated it for Christmas 1951.[5]

__Author's Connection:__ WLW had been known as the "Nation's Station" because its powerful towers created a huge listening audience across the nation. Even though government regulation eventually reduced the station's power, WLW remained a leader in programming—especially live music—as it developed from radio into television programming. Although most of the station's live music was popular or country, it did recognize the quality of First Christian's musical forces and the excellent acoustics of the sanctuary for recording the Messiah *broadcast.*

Rosemary Clooney, Andy Williams, and Nick Clooney were just a few whose early careers involved WLW. There were also some famous "house bands," two of which included the Chubb-Steinberg Orchestra of the 1920s and 1930s, and the Cliff Lash Orchestra in the 1950s, 60s, and 70s. Lash became famous through his work on Ruth Lyons' 50-50 Club broadcast, a show which was very popular on television.

Jack Saatkamp, jazz pianist for the Chubb-Steinberg band, was my piano teacher for a time when I was in late elementary school. He taught me to play chords with melodies and helped me to learn rudimentary concepts of improvisation through lead sheets he wrote out weekly, by hand. I still have many of them. Sadly, my study with him was cut short when he succumbed to cancer in 1958. I never fully appreciated all he taught me until I took music theory with Professor Berry at CBS. I already knew chords because of Jack Saatkamp. Such knowledge made music theory much easier for me, and I was ahead of the class. Of course, I had studied music theory in high school, too.

First Christian's successful *Messiah* broadcast caught the attention of the director of *The Christian's Hour* radio program. This program was produced by Restoration Movement congregations and has existed in some form from 1943 to the present day.[6] It featured preaching of Ard Hoven, who became preacher for First Christian Church in 1966. The listening audience for *The Christian's Hour* was estimated to be over one million (very significant for that time in history), and the church's choir became the broadcast choir for the program, beginning in March 1951.[7] From 1951 until the mid-1970s, the choir—or a select ensemble from the choir— recorded music for *The Christian's Hour*.[8] The main challenge for Berry and the choir was to limit music selections to public domain hymns. There was no budget for royalties for specific arrangements or copyrighted music. Such restrictions placed great creative pressure on musicians.

Centennial Celebrations

By 1952, the Christian Church was preparing to celebrate its one hundredth anniversary as a congregation. Several musical events were presented. After all, this church was not just influential in Columbus, and in Indiana, going back to John Fassett and Benjamin Irwin. It had a national and somewhat international reputation, too, because of Z. T. Sweeney, who spread its fame throughout the nation and outside the United States—even to Europe and Constantinople.

The first centennial event took place May 11, 1952. NBC broadcast the choir's presentation of Mendelssohn's oratorio, *St. Paul.*[9] Guy Owen Baker, nationally famous tenor soloist, and W. M. Johansen, equally famous bass, were guest soloists.[10] Other soloists, as well as soloists for most radio broadcasts, were from the choir's membership. Professor George Wilson of Indiana University was the organist for the oratorio, and Wayne Berry conducted.

Berry's former organ professor at Westminster, and co-designer of the church's organ, Carl Weinrich, presented an organ recital to a crowd of over nine hundred at the Christian Church one week later, on May 18, 1952. He concluded his program with the Third Movement from *The Ascension* by Messiaen, a daring finale for a small midwestern city in 1952. That same day, T. K. Smith and the congregation's choir were featured in a nationwide NBC broadcast called *Faith in Action.*[11]

The preceding one hundred years saw this congregation grow musically—from A. D. Fillmore's singing school and Joseph I. Irwin's song leading—to nationwide broadcast of acclaimed sanctuary, organ, and choir on NBC. That's a lot for Midwest Columbus, Indiana, to celebrate. The church's music aired regularly on radio and was featured on two televised programs.

Members of the congregation put together a pageant depicting the congregation's history and presented it twice during centennial week festivities, on May 20 and 21, 1952.[12] Most of the pageant was written by Hazel Crouch and featured descendants of early congregational leaders portraying their ancestors. The pageant script still exists in the church library. For the closing centennial service, on Sunday, June 1, 1952, Gladys and Hazel Payne led congregational singing and provided special music.[13]

A Theological Split

Ironically, shortly after the wonderful centennial celebrations, The Christian Church suffered the most difficult time in its entire history, culminating in a split. Issues had been brewing among Restoration Movement congregations for some time, and the specific ones which caused dissent at Columbus involved the role of women and mode of baptism according to the Scriptures.

The split, which began in late in 1952, was finalized by October 1955. The congregation which had been known as the Christian Church now became designated officially as First Christian Church.[14] The new congregation that split off became known as North Christian Church. J. Irwin Miller and forty families formed the nucleus for the new congregation. Despite the loss of many key members, First Christian Church remained the largest Restoration Movement congregation in Indiana and one of the largest in the nation.

North Christian Church affiliated itself with the Disciples of Christ—its agencies, missionary societies, and educational institutions, including Butler University's School of Religion. By 1964, North Christian Church moved into its new sanctuary designed by Eero Saarinen, son of Eliel Saarinen, who had designed First Christian's 1942 structure. J. Irwin Miller served as building committee chairman for North's building which included a Holtkamp pipe organ as part of the unique, contemporary design. Unfortunately, after many healthy years, the congregation dwindled and disbanded in the early 2020s after approximately seventy-five years of existence.

The church split took its toll on everyone, particularly friendships and musical collaborations, especially those of E. Wayne Berry, Edwin Crouch, and J. Irwin Miller. Edwin Crouch and J. Irwin Miller severed their professional relationship at Cummins, and Crouch re-established his private law practice, a practice which became quite successful and enabled him to fund significant monetary gifts to worthy institutions—including First Christian Church and the Cincinnati Bible Seminary.

Landmark musical partnerships between Wayne Berry and the Irwin-Sweeney-Miller family ended. Nettie died in 1960. Elsie Sweeney, while maintaining her Bible School class at First Christian, turned most of her musical attention to Indiana University. Clementine Miller spent most of her time in New York City with her husband, Robert Tangeman, whom she married in 1951.

Edwin G. Crouch and J. Irwin Miller assumed prominent leadership in their respective church organizations: Miller helped establish the National Council of Churches and was the organization's first lay-president from 1960-1963; Crouch was the first non-preacher to be elected president of the North American Christian Convention in 1960.

Crouch had become a trustee of the Cincinnati Bible Seminary and later chairman of the board. It was Crouch who influenced E. Wayne Berry to develop a comprehensive church music program at CBS, beginning with his part-time hiring in 1953. Berry resigned from First Christian Church in 1966 to become full-time at CBS. Crouch's untimely death in 1962 paved the way for his widow, Hazel, to be appointed as the first female trustee of the Cincinnati Bible Seminary.[15]

Around the time of Edwin's death, he and Hazel had gifted CBS one of the earliest Allen Electronic Organ installations in Cincinnati for the seminary's chapel at Price and Grand avenues in Price Hill. The three-manual installation was considered "top-of-the-line" as an electronic organ (even though this instrument was designed before digital technology was adapted to electronic organs). The organ's sound fooled many pipe-organ enthusiasts, who thought they were hearing authentic pipe sound.

The Cincinnati Bible Seminary constructed a library/graduate school building in 1968 and named it for Edwin Crouch.

Author's Reflection: As an undergraduate CBS student I sang in concert choir for dedication services held inside the Edwin G. Crouch building before it was filled with books. I also took part in moving the complete undergraduate library from the third floor of Old Main to the new facility.

Classes were cancelled and the entire student body was organized into groups to carry books in an orderly fashion across campus. Moving day began early with a devotional service in the chapel where instructions were given by librarian Victor Maxey. Professor Berry was seated at the organ during the entire service and could be seen by the entire audience. Mr. Maxey, in giving prolonged, awkward moving instructions was hilarious—without intending to be. It was the only time I ever witnessed Professor Berry lose his cool at the organ. While the audience laughed until they cried, Professor Berry laughed so hard we thought he was going to fall off the organ bench.

Years after Edwin's death, Hazel Crouch gave First Christian a set of handbells and a Baldwin Grand Piano for the sanctuary. The Crouches' monetary resources may not have equaled the Irwin-Sweeney-Miller's, but they definitely followed the example of Columbus's leading musical and educational philanthropic family. E. Wayne Berry reaped the benefit of association with both generous families and their musical inclinations. It is sad that close friends went separate ways in the theological realm, yet each of these three maintained their desire to fund musical projects in their spheres of influence.

Berry's Focus Shifts

As mentioned above, Berry accepted Edwin Crouch's challenge to expand the CBS music department. At first, he spent two days a week in Cincinnati and continued to teach at Butler University and Franklin College. For two years he drove over 500 miles a week to maintain his teaching schedule at all three colleges.[16] The routine involved one day at Butler, three days at Franklin, and two in Cincinnati. Later, as the work progressed at CBS, Berry resigned his position at Butler. By the 1960s he also left Franklin College and concentrated on work at First Christian and CBS. Such a rigorous schedule divided Berry's attention and sapped his creative energy. He maintained the program in Columbus, but with less creative innovation than in the past.

In the early days of teaching at CBS, Berry used the church choir in Columbus to augment his choirs in Cincinnati for the closing night's concert of the seminary's Conference on Evangelism (a large, three-day conference presented each fall at Taft Auditorium in downtown Cincinnati). There was always significant cooperation between First Christian and CBS. The Payne Sisters usually led singing for the Conference on Evangelism, which drew hundreds of people from all over the country.

T. K. Smith, First Christian's minister, was also a trustee at the seminary, and Frances Berry taught some voice students. As the music program at the seminary strengthened, Berry used personnel from the school as soloists with his church choir in Columbus—just the reverse of what he had to do early on. His concert choir from CBS performed at First Christian; one of the first such programs occurred April 2, 1954, during spring tour.[17] Obviously, he was always welcome to feature his choirs at home.

Berry's Last Decade at First Christian

The church's music program from the mid-1950s throughout the mid-1960s continued to include a children's choir, high school choir (later a girl's high school choir), and the adult choir. The adult choir provided most of the regular service music, but did not sing as many anthems each service as it had in the 1940s. Also, music for evening services was performed more often by smaller groups, soloists, and octet chosen from the adult choir.[18] The choir presented major Christmas programs, Easter programs, and participated in some combined concerts with other Columbus churches; however, there was not as much concert work by the mid-1950s. Wayne Berry continued to present occasional organ recitals, but his energy was increasingly focused on CBS. Although Professor George Wilson (I.U. Music faculty member who had participated in the centennial celebration services) was a guest organ recitalist on May 17, 1959,[19] and string and brass players from the university were still used occasionally, cooperative efforts between First Christian and Indiana University gradually ceased.

Church music in general, throughout the entire USA, remained strong in the 1950s and 60s; it was probably at its peak for the twentieth century. However, very definite changes were on the horizon. First Christian's historic traditional music ministry was not affected for a long time. Eventually, however, the traditional/contemporary worship wars did come to Columbus, too.

Major choral works presented in the last decade of Berry's leadership included "The Crucifixion" by John Steiner, "The Eternal Light" and "Gethsemane to Golgotha" by H. Alexander Matthew's, "For Us a Child is Born" (attributed at J. S. Bach at that time), *Christmas Oratorio* by J. S. Bach, *St. Paul* by Mendelssohn, *The Holy City* by Gaul and several portions of Handel's *Messiah*. Activities of the choir during Berry's last two years are chronicled in two pamphlets; *Chancel Choir Annuals* for 1964-65 and 1965-66.[20] These pamphlets indicated the choir organization and spiritual focus. They also included names and addresses of choir members, as well as interesting historical data.

At the close of 1965, T. K. Smith concluded a very fruitful preaching ministry with First Christian Church, which had lasted thirty-five years. For almost all of T. K.'s association with the congregation, Wayne Berry had been involved with the music program. Dr. Ard Hoven succeeded T. K. Smith as senior minister early in 1966.[21] By the spring of 1966, Wayne Berry decided to resign his position at the church and move to Cincinnati. He had been involved in a paid capacity at First Christian Church since 1925–the longest tenure of any paid staff member in the church's history. Berry devoted full-time attention to Cincinnati Bible Seminary's music department as department chairman until his retirement in 1974.

Farewell to E. Wayne Berry

For E. Wayne Berry's farewell party in the spring of 1966, five members of the adult choir—Margaret Dismore, Jane Allison, Mary Rogers, George Chandler, and Don Sandlin, with Ray Hass from the Presbyterian Church accompanying—presented J. S. Bach's *Coffee Cantata* ("Schweitzer stille, plaudert nicht", BWV 211) for a portion of the program. The secular cantata is loosely translated, "Be still, stop chattering," and is about a disgruntled father and his caffeine-obsessed daughter. The ensemble had great fun performing "the lighter side" of Bach; they wore costumes and repeated their memorable performance for other occasions in the city.[22]

I can't imagine how difficult the decision to leave Columbus must have been; yet Berry's influence continued to grow and reach a different audience—future musicians, teachers, and leaders in churches.

During his CBS years, Berry oversaw development of undergraduate and graduate degrees in music. His new musical platform had its own challenges, but he accepted them and still exerted quite an influence. He no longer had outstanding facilities which First Christian possessed. Many of his students, though aware of his high standards, were mostly unaware of all he had accomplished during more than forty years in Columbus, Indiana. Those who knew him best became most impressed by his integrity, kindness, and reluctance to be seen in the spotlight. He was truly a gentleman. He was not a temperamental musician by any standards, and his music grew out of a desire to be a faithful steward of God's amazing gifts and opportunities.

__Author's comment__: I earned four music degrees from three institutions, with more than fifty years' experience in college music education and music ministry in six states. I studied under and worked with exceptionally talented and highly trained singers, instrumentalists, conductors, *professors, general music teachers, and excellent professional and amateur musicians. In comparison, Professor Berry's character and musical pedigree ranked him with the best-of-the-best, but it took some time for me to fully recognize how exceptional he was. Furthermore, I can count on one hand the number of professionals with similar length, depth, and variety of professional experience in their careers. Columbus, Indiana, should be proud of their hometown boy-to-man, who started as organist at First Presbyterian—age thirteen—and left First Christian—age fifty-six.*

In my undergraduate experience, if you came to a class or lesson with Professor Berry ill-prepared, it was not likely he would scold or tongue-lash, and I don't remember him losing his temper with choirs or individuals. He was more likely to become quieter and let piano and organ students plow-through a poorly prepared, unpracticed selection, during which he might squirm, wiggle his jaw, but let students suffer and sweat it out as they tried to get through the ordeal they had put themselves in. Such an experience was utterly exhausting, and—from my perspective—more likely to motivate increased practice in the future, than if he had yelled, belittled, and lectured as many other music teachers are prone to do. He really was a class act in every way.

According to calculations from information he shared, Professor Berry taught at Franklin College for approximately twenty years, was special lecturer in church music at Butler University for about twenty years, and taught at Cincinnati Bible Seminary for twenty-one years. He made quite an impact on music and musicians wherever he served. Although he remembered and recalled his amazing musical years in Columbus, he did not seem the least bit sad about leaving those years of exceptional accomplishment behind. He remained focused on his current music-making and his current students. As he gradually had more time, Berry began to compose and arrange more music—choral, piano, and some organ compositions, too. I remember him saying that he was rather annoyed he had to "practice his own compositions" to get the music "in his fingers." Just because he wrote it didn't mean he could automatically play it.

1. "Church Choir," *A Century 1852-1952*, [n. p].
2. Sunday morning bulletin, April 9, 1950.
3. Printed program from concert.
4. Survey of Sunday morning bulletins from 1948-1952.
5. Sunday morning bulletin, December 2, 1951. Instrumentalists from Indiana University assisted, and the program was recorded on December 9.
6. www.oneplace.com. The Christians Hour.
7. "Centennial Program Christian Church 1852-1952," *The Evening Republican*, May 16, 1952.

8. Survey of *The Carillon* articles throughout 1970s.
9. "Church Choirs," *A Century*, [n. p.].
10. Printed program "Centennial Services 1852-1952."
11. "Centennial Program of Christian Church 1852-1952," *The Evening Republican*, May 16, 1952.
12. Printed program "Centennial Services"
13. Ibid.
14. Telephone conversation with Margaret Dismore on February 11, 1989.
15. Telephone conversation with Earl Sims, Vice-President for Academic Affairs at Cincinnati Bible College and Seminary, February 16, 1989.
16. Telephone conversation with E. Wayne Berry on January 24, 1989.
17. Printed program.
18. Survey of Sunday morning bulletins throughout the years of E. Wayne Berry's leadership. The bulletins contained morning and evening orders of worship.
19. Sunday morning bulletin, May 17, 1959.
20. Survey of Sunday morning bulletins, 1956-1966.
21. *Chancel Choir Annuals* were loaned to the author from E. Wayne Berry for study in August 1988.
22. Sunday morning bulletin, January 2, 1966.
23. Questionnaire from Margaret Dismore, p. 2, and information from concert program.

Chapter Nine: Fruition and Change

The mid-to-late 1950s and early 1960s saw continued expansion in Columbus's musical, theatrical, and worship offerings. As in the rest of the country, popular music was booming, entertainment possibilities were increasing, and yet, serious, classical music still found a prominent place. By 1966—the concluding date for this historical account—revolutions in Christian music, counterculture, and worship styles were just starting to "hit the fan." Terms like Jesus Movement, British Invasion, classic rock, pop, and soul were emerging; disco, rap, funk, punk, hip-hop, and new age were poised to knock us off our feet. In the mid-'60s, how little we understood what computers, the Internet, and cell phones would do to revolutionize all our music, not to mention every aspect of life. Let's briefly ponder some musical entertainment life in Columbus of the mid-twentieth century.

In 1947, two Barbour brothers, Don and Ross, from Columbus reunited after World War II as students at Butler University's Arthur Jordan Conservatory of Music and formed a quartet. Don and Ross had sung with their parents, Maude and Harold Barbour, while growing up in a musi-

The Four Freshmen. // Bartholomew County Historical Society

cal family. In college the Barbour brothers together with a cousin, Bill Flanigan, from Greencastle—who contributed an amazing high tenor voice and had taken the place of fellow music student, Marvin Pruitt— to form a group first known as The Toppers ... then The Four Freshmen in 1948. Their sound marked a huge transition in popular music from barbershop harmonies of the Mel-tones, Modernaires, and Pied Pipers to sounds of The Beach Boys. Brian Wilson freely admitted he was influenced by The Four Freshmen—their sound, jazz harmonies, and interpretations.[1]

The Four Freshmen sang five-part harmony and created "purple chords"— so they called them—deep, warm, and rich. Whatever you called it, their sound created a standard which paved the way for noteworthy groups of the near future, such as The Lettermen, The Association, and Manhattan Transfer. Four Freshmen hits included "It's a Blue World," "Candy," "Mood Indigo," and "Graduation Day." Capitol Records established a successful ten-year recording contract with the group, and they were nominated for six Grammys.[2] Columbus was proud of them; the Four Freshmen appeared in Columbus Jaycees' Spring Series on April 19, 1956, along with Nat King Cole and the Ted Heath band.[3]

Between 1955 and 1960, the Jaycees' (Junior Chamber of Commerce) Auditorium Series brought many nationally known musicians to town. The list included Eydie Gormè, Fred Waring and his Pennsylvanians, Bob Hope, Arthur Fiedler and the Boston Pops Orchestra, Guy Lombardo's Royal Canadians, flamenco dancer Josè Greco, and Louis Armstrong.[4] (I'm sure there were more.) Patricia M. Mote's book, *Images of America: Columbus*, includes a picture from December 7, 1957, of a performance at Columbus High School's Memorial Gymnasium.[5] Such concerts were very well-attended and provided diverse musical programs. Columbus had enjoyed quality musical entertainment for more than one hundred years, and its artistic leaders continued to maintain this benefit to the community.

Gary F. Davis Sr. became director for the City Band's first concert series in 1952 after an eighteen-year absence from the Columbus musical scene.[6] He had played with many groups, including the Columbus Symphony. He remained as conductor of the concert series until 1959, while having established his Music Makers Store in 1957 as a hobby. However, his hobby soon turned into an actual store in 1959, named for his Music Makers band which existed from 1946-1960. The Music Makers were available to play dances and floor shows.

During the 1960s, and into the 1970s, WCSI radio broadcast a jazz program hosted by Bill McCoy. McCoy's real name was George William "Bill" Kitzinger (1943-2012), son of G. Chester Kitzinger, founder of the

G. Chester Kitzinger with high school band members. // Bartholomew
County Historical Society

Columbus Symphony. McCoy hosted some of the early Columbus Jazz
Festival presentations, too.

Meanwhile, the local symphony orchestra had its ups and downs, but persevered. Regular programming ceased in 1954 for several years. At the
May 3, 1954, concert, Dorothy Munger returned to Columbus as guest pianist and featured soloist from the Indianapolis Symphony. She performed
on a Steinway grand as part of the special Steinway Centennial Concert
celebrating the piano maker's one-hundred-year history.

That night's audience didn't realize it would be more than sixteen years
until the orchestra would play together again. In a strange way, the growth
of Columbus hastened the demise of the orchestra; people had more op-
tions on Sunday afternoon, causing rehearsal attendance to dwindle.[7] The
orchestra also lost its rehearsal space at the Chamber of Commerce when
it moved. Kitzinger, ever resourceful, organized the Singing Strings, twen-

ty-two musicians from the string section, who, over the next fifteen years, played about sixty concerts. G. Chester Kitzinger's perseverance was certainly noteworthy.

In 1970 the Columbus Pro Musica was founded to re-establish the Columbus Symphony.[8] Patricia M. Mote's book points out the Columbus Symphony was not only the oldest symphony in the state (formed in 1922), but it also was the first for a city the size of Columbus at this time in the USA.[9] The symphony enjoyed increased support and growth during the last part of the twentieth century. A bright future was secured for this pioneering musical ensemble. As a tribute to its grassroots success and G. Chester Kitzinger's leadership, the symphony's files listed around 500 musicians who had played in the volunteer ensemble through the years. The shear number of names indicates the firm cultural foundation and musical strength of Columbus, Indiana.

Situation When Wayne Berry Closed Columbus Career

By the time E. Wayne Berry left in 1966 to teach at Cincinnati Bible Seminary, his concert activity had slowed significantly. His 1940s and '50s musical golden age at First Christian Church had dimmed, and his attention was consumed with developing a quality music department at CBS. His cutting-edge music venue and organ had become normal for regular programming at church. There were no more jaw-dropping musical projects funded by Irwin-Sweeney-Miller money. Nettie died in 1960. Clementine's life was more connected to New York City and the Union Theological Seminary School of Sacred Music after Robert Tangeman's early death in 1964. Elsie's attention became focused on designing and building her elegant, new home, Castelia, and supporting Indiana University's School of Music—though she still taught her Sunday School class as long as she could, until her death in 1972.

J. Irwin Miller's decision to leave First Christian Church had ended more than one hundred and twenty years of significant family involvement—his business and ecumenical endeavors became both monumental and incredibly successful. He became quite active in civil rights and politics, and was even talked about as a possible presidential candidate in 1968.[10]

Berry claimed his friendship with J. Irwin existed until Berry left Columbus, but, as I said in an earlier chapter, I detected it was never really the same between them. I never heard Berry say anything against his childhood friend. The Cincinnati Bible Seminary became a much more biblically conservative school than Butler University's School of Religion, which morphed into Christian Theological Seminary. This theological reality, more than any other, accounts for the unfortunate cooling of a life-long friendship. No one seemed to foresee (or have a remedy for) such a sad development.

However, what an incredibly rich (literally and figuratively) relationship E. Wayne Berry enjoyed in the Columbus musical world because of the support given so generously by the Irwin-Sweeney-Miller family. Berry enjoyed long, close ties with Linnie, W. G., Nettie, Hugh Th., J. Irwin, and Clementine for over four decades.

Remaining Questions

Naturally, I am left with unanswered questions and contemplations, and I have no more living resources to consult. Availability of old newspapers online has been invaluable. The Internet is wonderful for research, but it is limited. "Why?" "What?" "Give me more details!" These are all questions which have consumed me at times.

Surely someone will continue the musical story from 1966 to the present-day. Columbus musicians, historians, and writers—this is your task. Who will take it up? Someone should continue the story (many stories) from 1966 onward. There is still much to share about music in Columbus, Indiana. Many talented people have contributed greatly.

Early in our marriage, Katie and I mused why Professor Berry hired her— right out of graduate school—to teach music theory and piano. She was overwhelmed at times. She did not have college-teaching experience, and had a few "hard nuts to crack" among her early students. I used to say—in addition to a lower salary—Berry saw benefit in a young Katie, someone easier to mold into what he wanted. (Yes, I have repented I ever thought this thought.)

After researching, thinking, and writing, I grew to modify my assertion: E. Wayne Berry saw in Katie someone with spunk, somewhat like Elsie and Nettie. I think he saw someone who would give her all to the calling; and he was exactly on target. Although Dr. Katie Cartwright completed a fifty-one-year career teaching music theory and piano to college students, she continues today, in retirement, to teach piano and tutor music theory students from our Lanett, Alabama, home. (Elsie, Nettie, Benjamin Hutchins, Jessie Kitchen, and Will Harding, too—would be proud.) I would also be remiss if I did not also say Professor Berry was a patient musical mentor to Katie.

I have wondered many times if E. Wayne Berry ever got tired of Nettie and Elsie directing his every musical move. Even though the sisters provided great blessings, they surely meddled musically. Did he pursue HIS heart's desire in music? He never let on if, indeed, his was a mixed bag of blessings. Berry's interaction with W. G., Linnie, Elsie, Hugh Th., Nettie, Clementine, and J. Irwin was simply astounding and produced incredible musical results—remarkable on so many levels. Berry never hinted at any misgivings concerning the bountiful musical projects the Irwin-Sweeney-Miller family bestowed on him. I have a challenge for all musicians: Identify your musical benefactors and mentors and thank them for their investment in you.

Other Musings

I knew about singing schools in the early United States. Dr. Hugh McElrath at Southern Seminary opened the door to my appreciation of this American phenomenon when I took his course, "Music in the United States," in 1979. A. D. Fillmore certainly set the stage—with Joseph I. Irwin—for the musical future of Columbus, Indiana. Fillmore's singing school lessons yielded great long-term dividends for generations. I was able to research and discover what singing schools contributed to the development of music in America by chronicling what took place in Columbus; and, again, I say confidently, it was amazing.

I was fascinated by William and Jennie Bates and wish I could find out more about them—I tried. Jennie was conducting a church choir of adult men and women in the nineteenth century—amazing. I really came to admire Benjamin M. Hutchins and all that he did, especially in music education—what a multi-talented, influential man he was. He gave so much to his community and helped bring East-Coast musical culture to the Midwest through Artemas Nixon Johnson, whose influence bore significant fruit.

To think that G. Chester Kitzinger could establish a community symphony orchestra by building on a small Sunday School orchestra and incorporating members of Gary F. Davis' city band demonstrates true talent, patience, and great fortitude. What incredible blessings these two men brought to instrumental musical life in Columbus.

First Christian Church hired qualified musicians (though often in their twenties) who had a spiritual dimension to their music. Furthermore, the congregation's musical staff throughout history was always very active in the community, not defined by church programming only. It was interesting to see how the congregation's young musicians created quite an impact, and I didn't see that any were destroyed by perennial problems of the complicated church world. I love to see churches and schools contribute to the music of a community—together.

I have the benefit of knowing that First Christian Church and Columbus, Indiana, continued their amazing musical past into their present, and they have plans for the future. Current times call for communal musical expression in all contexts of life—education, worship, and entertainment—for emotional and intellectual health, not to mention exercise of God-given creativity. Music is a powerful tool of universal communication, and needs emphasis in the heart of all communities.

Thank you, Columbus, Indiana, for your rich, amazing musical story. I hope others are motivated to share musical gifts with their communities. I'm glad this southern transplant had opportunity to probe and share his Midwest roots. I've been incredibly blessed.

__Author's Afterthought:__ In response to conversations and emails about completing this book, I have been reminded of a noteworthy facet of E. Wayne Berry's CBS legacy, a facet that needs proper emphasis. One could say Berry's legacy had been rehearsed for more than forty years in Columbus before finding its fruition in Cincinnati. Thorough re-evaluation prompts me to realize the information below is not afterthought, but forms the crux of thrilling blessings hundreds received through what I designate simply as "chapel music" at CBS.

Upon my arrival at college, age eighteen, in September 1967, I began to experience congregational singing that would transform my life and future ministry. Anywhere from 300 to 500 students and faculty attended chapel services; they walked several blocks from the main campus or piled in vehicles, as many as would fit, to attend worship voluntarily twice each week—no required chapel. Professor Berry usually accompanied at the organ after playing a prelude. Although he never said a word, he had a way of making sure the congregation got immediately quiet as he began the prelude. Professor Roy Koerner then led the hymns. Roy had a powerful bass voice, but it really was not necessary for him to sing or conduct, even though he did both extremely well. Professor Berry's organ skill was all that was necessary to lead the congregation—and oh, did the congregation sing! Everyone participated, and even though some complained about the standard hymnody we used—instead of only the gospel hymns they knew from their home churches— people sang quite exuberantly. The volume, energy, and whole-hearted participation were absolutely breathtaking. EVERY-ONE, not just musicians and music lovers, commented on the power and vitality of the congregational singing. I never remember anyone not singing. It was truly a spiritual experience, and I didn't fully understand for years how much Professor Berry's organ playing helped to create, convey, and underscore the spiritual message of the texts and music. Martin Luther was right: "Next to the Word of God, music deserves the highest praise."

I thought I appreciated organ music before this; my mother had played organ for church. But Professor Berry's choice of music and artistic per-formances were on a level I had never experienced before. I heard him play for chapel for eight years through spring 1974, when he retired. To this day, the memories of his music bless my soul. Those memories speak to me when I recall praise, exhortation, penitence, and comfort. Berry played a variety of preludes, including hymn tunes and classical works. Two that stand out in my mind are "Aria" by Flor Peeters and "Carol Rhapsody" by Richard Purvis. To this day, I play performances on YouTube of these favorites. At the conclusion of every chapel service, Berry played a very brief organ response to the benediction; he had an uncanny gift for choosing an appropriate phrase from a hymn that would unite the congregation with the spoken message of the service as we concluded. Following Berry's retirement, one of his outstanding students who taught on faculty, Mary Ann Jordan, continued the organ tradition. Later, one of Mary Ann Jordan's outstanding students, Don Seevers, joined the faculty and continued the organ tradition.

As far as the hymns Berry accompanied using the Columbus hymnal Christian Hymns, *I will never forget "Thy Hand, O God, Has Guid-ed" (text: Edward H. Plumptre, music: Basil Harwood) and "Who is on the Lord's Side" (text: Frances R. Havergal, music: John Goss). And the way he could present accompaniment to "Marching to Zion" (text: Isaac Watts, music: Robert Lowry) with such a vibrant, rollicking quality for the 6/8 tune, it was impossible for the congregation to sing lethargically.*

Occasionally, people today heap criticism on the organ and church or-ganists. I respond, saying that if you have a sensitive, gifted organist and a quality instrument housed within fine acoustical setting, then you can experience glorious, varied organ music in worship. During the last few decades of my college teaching career, when my music students, immersed in contemporary praise bands, were exposed for the first time to a fine organ played by a fine organist, their eyes, imaginations, and souls literally lit up. They had no idea what they had been missing.

1. fourfreshmen.com. Indy Star "Retro Indy: The Four Freshmen began at Butler University, February 10, 2017.

2. Ibid.

3. Patricia M. Mote, *Images of America Columbus*, Charleston, South Carolina: Arcadia Publishing, 2005, p. 127.

4. Ibid.

5. Ibid.

6. newspapers.com. "Music Makers," by Kelli Rowe, p. 22.

7. *The Republic*, "Changing Times hit Columbus Symphony Orchestra," by Jean Prather, Monday, October 13, 1967, p. 8.

8. Patricia Mote's, p. 124.

9. Ibid.

10. Rentschler, p. 105.

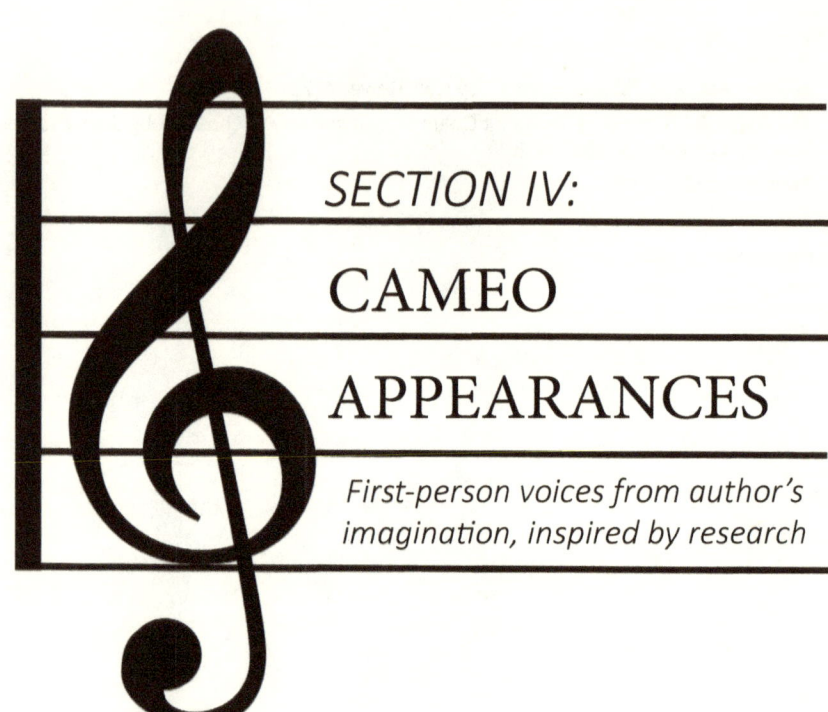

SECTION IV:

CAMEO
APPEARANCES

*First-person voices from author's
imagination, inspired by research*

Chapter Ten: Joseph Irwin Introduces His Family

There have been many articles written about me and especially my successful business ventures during the mid-to-late 19th-century days of Bartholomew County, Indiana. However, I want to give you my perspective and introduce my entire family.

Shortly after arriving in Columbus in 1846, I turned twenty-two. Indiana was a very different place from today, and I was a very different man from the one who saw the twentieth century dawn before my death in 1910. In my earliest memories, farms, dirt roads, blacksmiths, and horsepower dominated daily life. I knew adults who could recall when Indiana became a state and scattered Indian tribes remained. The wildness of the county was quickly tamed, but it was still much less civilized and cultured than Columbus became—just a couple of decades later.

Joseph Irwin //
Bartholomew County
Historical Society

I was very poor, with very little experience, except for work on my father's farm. My father had died, and I needed to provide more for my mother than was possible on our little farm. Even working on Uncle Benjamin's successful farm did not hold the promise I saw in moving to the village of Columbus. Although there were no mansions, large churches, grand public buildings, and thriving businesses, everyone worked hard just to get-by in our energetic town. We all believed in the future of our community and nation. We shared our labor, our love, our food, and our faith in the future—there was no time for frivolous behavior. My family was frugal and God-fearing, avoiding liquor, tobacco, gambling, and dangerous excesses. We preached against such sins.

We were very much opposed to slavery, too, even though many in Bartholomew County were southern sympathizers. Although it had been determined there would be no slavery in the Northwest Territory, the subject

The Irwin home in the 1870s. // Bartholomew County Historical Society

caused division until after the War Between the States. Our family solidly supported Ovid Butler's plans as an abolitionist in starting the university which came to bear his name, but sometimes it was not easy. My opposition to slavery once provoked a threat upon my life.

Church was very important in our lives. Our worship was simple. The Bible was our foundation, and we sang songs most of us already knew. Instruments were quite few in both number and variety. Those of us with Scottish and Irish roots drew upon texts and tunes passed on to us in our families. We loved to sing, and little by little our singing improved, especially when singing schools came to town. My work in the dry goods store gave me concrete hope in the future, more money in my pocket, and I saved every penny I possibly could.

But a singing school at New Hope Church refreshed my spirit after days of hard work; it opened my eyes to the joy, beauty, and power of music, and cultivated my natural love of singing. I'll always be thankful for what I learned about music from my friend, A. D. Fillmore, in his singing school. People took note of my natural singing voice, and soon I put into weekly use all the singing school taught me. I led music at New Hope Church and joined with the congregation that established itself in Columbus. There I took charge of singing, too, and continued to do so for more than twenty-five years.

It's hard to believe, now, how quickly my circumstances improved. People grew to respect me, even as I bought more and more land that became the heart of our town of Columbus; I sold off lots for houses as the town grew. I opened my own store, and people began trusting me to keep their money in my store safe. There was only one other bank in town; it was a national bank where Randolph Griffith was president and Francis J. Crump, an equally community-minded, trustworthy gentleman, started out as vice president. Francis and I wanted to see our town thrive, and we invested in projects to make a better community.

Harriet Glanton Irwin //
Bartholomew County
Historical Society

No doubt, you will associate the Crump name with his Opera Hall built in 1872, and later, the theater his son, John S. Crump, built. My financial organization was soon chartered as a bank under the private banking laws of Indiana. With the establishment of my bank, Columbus had two trustworthy financial institutions. Not all communities could make that assertion; our banks survived hard economic times, and we treated people fairly. We served our community well.

I married Harriet Clementine Glanton on August 15, 1850. She was an excellent wife who ran a wonderful home, and our lives were busy at home and church. Even when some of my influential, powerful friends, like Abraham Lincoln and Benjamin Harrison, suggested political positions which would have added to my fame and prestige, I wanted to make my mark in Indiana—in Columbus. This was my home and I loved it. I was very involved in building the Christian Chapel in 1852, which was large and exceptional for its day. More and more lovely, spacious homes seemed to just spring-up in town, and in 1864–despite the Civil War—I was able to build my Harriet a modest home on the corner of Fifth Avenue and Mechanic (now Lafayette) Street. I improved and enlarged our home at least twice, as our family grew and generations moved in with us. Years later, Will, my son, renovated his third-floor quarters and added magnificent gardens.

As a leading citizen of the community, I entered into many projects for the progress of the town: a starch factory, interurban roads, telephone lines, to name a few. Of course, my personal financial situation improved as well. Making money seemed to come easily for me, but I always viewed my wealth as a tool to share a good life with others in church and communi-

Irwin-Sweeney-Miller Family Relationships & Musical Highlights

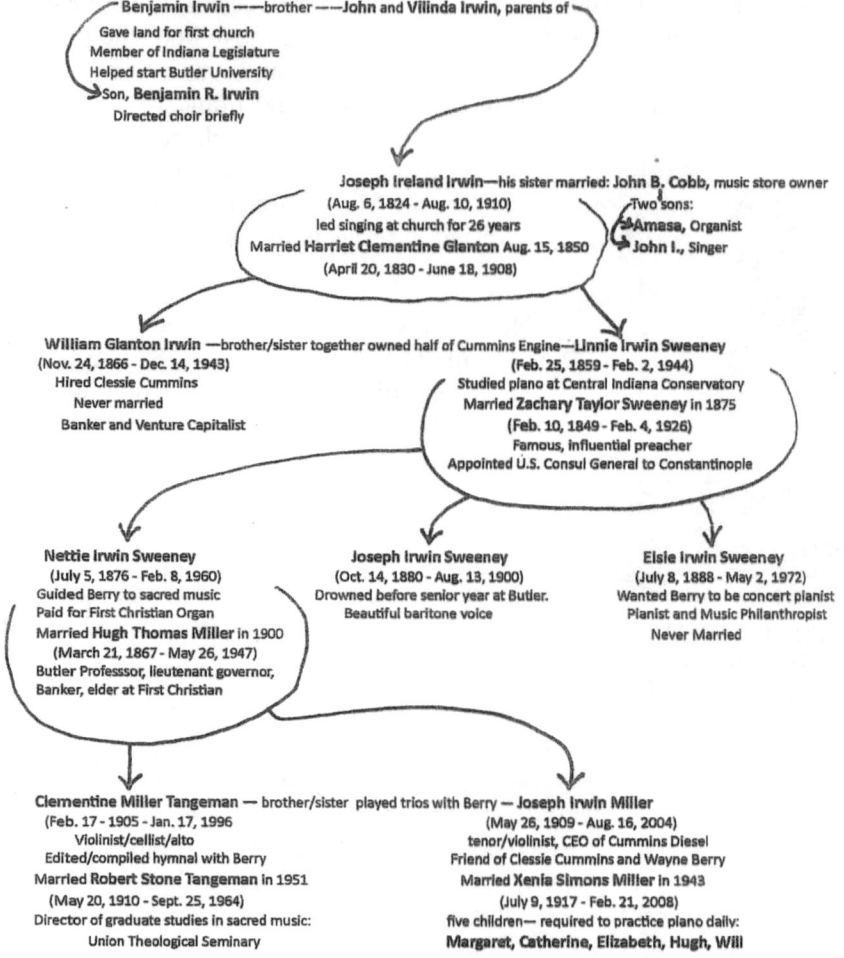

Benjamin Irwin ————brother————John and Vilinda Irwin, parents of ⤵
Gave land for first church
Member of Indiana Legislature
Helped start Butler University
⤷Son, Benjamin R. Irwin
Directed choir briefly

Joseph Ireland Irwin—his sister married: John B. Cobb, music store owner
(Aug. 6, 1824 - Aug. 10, 1910)
led singing at church for 26 years
Married Harriet Clementine Glanton Aug. 15, 1850
(April 20, 1830 - June 18, 1908)

Two sons:
⤷Amasa, Organist
⤷John I., Singer

William Glanton Irwin —brother/sister together owned half of Cummins Engine—Linnie Irwin Sweeney
(Nov. 24, 1866 - Dec. 14, 1943)
Hired Clessie Cummins
Never married
Banker and Venture Capitalist

(Feb. 25, 1859 - Feb. 2, 1944)
Studied piano at Central Indiana Conservatory
Married Zachary Taylor Sweeney in 1875
(Feb. 10, 1849 - Feb. 4, 1926)
Famous, influential preacher
Appointed U.S. Consul General to Constantinople

Nettie Irwin Sweeney
(July 5, 1876 - Feb. 8, 1960)
Guided Berry to sacred music
Paid for First Christian Organ
Married Hugh Thomas Miller in 1900
(March 21, 1867 - May 26, 1947)
Butler Professsor, lieutenant governor,
Banker, elder at First Christian

Joseph Irwin Sweeney
(Oct. 14, 1880 - Aug. 13, 1900)
Drowned before senior year at Butler.
Beautiful baritone voice

Elsie Irwin Sweeney
(July 8, 1888 - May 2, 1972)
Wanted Berry to be concert pianist
Pianist and Music Philanthropist
Never Married

Clementine Miller Tangeman — brother/sister played trios with Berry — Joseph Irwin Miller
(Feb. 17 - 1905 - Jan. 17, 1996)
Violinist/cellist/alto
Edited/compiled hymnal with Berry
Married Robert Stone Tangeman in 1951
(May 20, 1910 - Sept. 25, 1964)
Director of graduate studies in sacred music:
Union Theological Seminary

(May 26, 1909 - Aug. 16, 2004)
tenor/violinist, CEO of Cummins Diesel
Friend of Clessie Cummins and Wayne Berry
Married Xenia Simons Miller in 1943
(July 9, 1917 - Feb. 21, 2008)
five children— required to practice piano daily:
Margaret, Catherine, Elizabeth, Hugh, Will

Byron Cartwright

ty—so did my son, William Glanton Irwin, (known to most folks in town simply as "W. G."). He was quite the entrepreneur, inheriting the fortune I left him and growing it even larger.

Life was more than business, and I used my influence and wealth to help start the Central Indiana Conservatory of Music and build a grand Tabernacle Church of Christ with the largest pipe organ outside of Indianapolis. My family, and especially my descendants, viewed music as more than mere decoration in our lives; it was woven into the very fabric of who we were and what we chose to do. Harriet and I always supported musical endeavors.

When Benjamin Hutchins came to Columbus in 1872, I found a kindred soul for partnership in many of my loves; he, too, had a mind for business. I also realized it was time to turn over song-leading to him at church. He was younger and possessed a fine baritone voice. Benjamin wanted to bring a conservatory of music to Columbus from Madison, Indiana. I assisted in the project and enlisted the persuasive ability of my multi-talented son-in-law, Zachery Taylor Sweeney. He was a real "Cracker Jack" some would say, but also a positive influence as the effervescent, powerful preacher at Tabernacle Church of Christ.

More and more throughout my life, I used my money when finances became strained at church, and especially when the pipe organ needed repairs—pipe organs seemed to take a lot of money. Benjamin Hutchins and I kept our eyes on the church's music program so that it didn't suffer any more than was necessary through some hard times of recession and depression in the 1870s and 1890s.

I was blessed with a good life and devoted family. My descendants carried on and remained true to the values and priorities I believed in. Their successes greatly surpassed mine, even though by 1910 I was considered the wealthiest person in Indiana! Because all my family had such important associations with music in Columbus (and throughout the state and nation), it may be hard to keep them organized in your mind; therefore, I have included a musical family tree to consult as you read this book.

Perhaps, my greatest sorrow, however, also came through my family. Although my son Will never married, Linnie and Z.T. had three children: Nettie, Elsie, and a son, whom they named Joseph Irwin Sweeney in my honor. How proud I was. Nettie and Elsie became movers and shakers in their worlds, and young Joseph was on course to exert the same type of influence. He was handsome, had a great personality, was an excellent student at Butler University, possessed an excellent baritone voice and often performed solos. He organized and was elected president of the glee club at Butler, and president of his fraternity. So much promise. Such a busy boy … such a good boy.

A sudden turn of events changed everything on August 13, 1900. My family and many friends were invited to our golden wedding celebration at our Fifth Avenue home. We looked forward to a wonderful evening, however, when guests arrived, Harriet and I were the bearers of horrible news. Our only grandson, our beloved Joseph, had drowned while swimming in White River, near town, earlier that afternoon. He was ready for his senior year at Butler and was excited for his twentieth birthday in October. Immeasurable grief and sadness came over us. It was excruciatingly painful—ever so hard to bear. This untimely accident impacted our entire family for a long time. Although our Christian faith sustained us, and we eventually persevered and overcame, our hearts were broken for a loss which was unfathomable. We pressed on, trying not to live in the past.

My granddaughter, Nettie, and her husband, Hugh Th. Miller, wanted to honor me when their son was born a few years after their daughter Clementine. They named the boy Joseph Irwin Miller, and he fulfilled all the promise we felt when Joseph Irwin Sweeney was born, but it was just too difficult for our family to call Nettie and Hugh's boy "Joseph"— doing so recalled too much grief and pain. Therefore, he became known as "J. Irwin" during his entire life, and with that name, J. Irwin Miller, my great-grandson, left quite a legacy through Cummins Engine Company which he led to become Cummins Diesel, a very profitable worldwide corporation. His emphasis on great architecture also enriched our town tremendously and put Columbus on the map.

As you read this book, I hope you grow to love Columbus, my church, and my family. Harriet and I were the original Irwin matriarch/patriarch, then came the Sweeneys, and finally the Millers. Irwin-Sweeney-Miller family members loved this community and worked hard to provide a foundation on which residents could build quality lives.

Chapter Eleven: W. G. Irwin: 'Yes, I Do Belong in This Book!'

Please call me W. G.—everyone called me by my initials, except nieces and nephews, who just called me "Unk." My friends, you may never have thought of my life in Columbus, Indiana, as being connected to the musical world of community or state, but I want to let you know that my influence, money, and forethought have benefitted several musical stories in Columbus, Indiana, for generations—even today. Yes, I do belong in this book. Although I may not have had the beautiful voice of my father, Joseph Ireland Irwin, nor the musical ear of my sister, Linnie Irwin Sweeney, I did possess a discerning eye and ear for sharing beauty in the world around me.

I followed faithfully in the entrepreneurial footsteps of my father. Combining his love for the church and community, and all that benefits both, I spent my life as others have noted, "slaving for the Christian Church, working for the Republican Party, and playing at making money." I was blessed to inherit the fortune my father bequeathed to me—about five million dollars. I didn't have to start from scratch as he did. Furthermore, I can see that I was born at a time in American history when it was possible to make a lot of money, and therefore I used a lot of money to enrich the church and community. Today, I think you would call me a venture capitalist.

I also invested in creative people such as Clessie Cummins and Wayne Berry. When others brought me ideas for improved engines, new architecture, a fabulous organ, or new businesses, I recognized potential in their dreams and invested in future reality. Thus, my sister Linnie and I invested substantial funds in Clessie Cummins' ideas, even though it took many years to see a return. Also, in our wills, Linnie and I established trusts for future maintenance of First Christian Church and its organ.

If today's Cummins Inc. still makes engines, if you have attended worship or a concert at First Christian Church, if you have been stirred by the great organ at First Christian, studied church music under E. Wayne Berry, enjoyed programs presented by the oldest symphony in Indiana—here in Columbus—as well as the Indianapolis Symphony Orchestra, then I have given you a gift through my loves and financial investments. Please note that the list of institutions and programs which have benefitted from my philanthropy is incomplete; although there are more, I'll stop with those listed. But I challenge you to pass on the joy of your own gifts and investments. Be good stewards.

In closing, I leave you something I hope will thrill your soul. Please visit and enjoy the beautiful sunken gardens at The Inn at Irwin Gardens. I loved plants, trees, flowers, and horticultural wonders. The gardens I envisioned have been restored to their 1910 pristine state; they are adjacent to my family's mansion. The mansion, now a bed and breakfast, I greatly expanded in 1910, and it exists today with hardly any restoration. It is almost exactly as I left it in 1943. I encourage you to stroll through my gardens and

The Irwin Sweeney Gardens and house on July 22, 2021. // Byron Cartwright

to remember John Keats' words, which still ring true today, "A thing of beauty is a joy forever."

Chapter Twelve: Miss Elsie Sweeney Speaks

Thank you so much for wanting to meet me. I love people, and I love to share with them—especially my two great loves: my faith and my music. Daddy (Elder Z. T. Sweeney as he was known to most people) was a very powerful, influential preacher, and I was a member of his congregation, Tabernacle Church of Christ, all my life. (Well, later it became known as First Christian Church—but it will always be Tabernacle Church to me.) I taught a Bible School class for over fifty years. Yes, I traveled extensively—to Europe, and especially New York City—but I returned home as often as I could to teach my class at church. I guess you could say I preached to them; I inherited my father's gifts of communication and persuasion, and I was never at a loss for sharing my faith—or strong ideas.

My love of music was nurtured through my mother's side of the family. Grandaddy Irwin had a beautiful voice, and his daughter Linnie (my mother) encouraged my love for music from a very early age. People say I exhibited exceptional talent as a child. There are darling photographs of me singing in a children's quartet called the Little Giant Quartet for various occasions in the community. I think we sounded good? I can't imagine mother letting us sing unless we were exceptional. We were very young elementary-age singers, and I remember we had great fun performing.

Elsie Sweeney //
Bartholomew County
Historical Society

Mother taught me so much. She said I was one of those children who never had to be encouraged to practice. Indeed, I practiced the piano almost every day of my entire life. I believe it was a complete surprise to Sam Chizmar (organist/choir director at church) and his wife when I played Chopin's *Revolutionary Etude* following a dinner party I hosted. Yes, I was eighty-one years old, but I kept my piano technique in tip-top shape. You must remember that mother (Linnie Irwin Sweeney) had studied piano at the Central Indiana Conservatory of Music. I believe Professor William Bates was her teacher. Mother took her music very seriously, even though she never performed in public, and I inherited my musical drive

The Little Giant Quartet, also known as the Miniature Quartet, was composed of four Columbus, Indiana children under the age of 6. Elsie Irwin Sweeney is second from the right. The other members were Nell Burnett, Joe Bruce, and Bloor Schleppy. // Irwin-Sweeney-Miller Family Collection, Indiana Historical Society.

from her. Unfortunately, when the conservatory building was destroyed by fire in 1887, mother's piano study came to a halt. However, her love for and devotion to music continued for the rest of her life. She sponsored a children's choir at church for years—by doing so I believe she was memorializing my brother, Joseph, whose untimely death had devastated her.

I attended Smith College in Northampton, Massachusetts, and pursued music as my degree, majoring in piano. I accompanied the college glee club and for my senior piano recital, I performed a concerto with the college orchestra. I graduated in 1910.

Even though trouble in Europe was brewing which would lead to World War I in July 1914, mother and I spent the winter of 1913-1914 in Berlin so I could study piano with Josef Lhevinne, the Russian piano virtuoso. Because of the Russian Revolution and World War I, Lhevinne and his equally gifted wife, Rosina, could not leave Berlin. They lost everything when they left Russia, and they were not allowed to leave Berlin until after the Great War. As soon as possible, the Lhevinnes came to the United States. Together, they travelled the world concertizing and receiving rave reviews. Both joined the graduate piano faculty at Juilliard in 1924. They were fabulous pianists. Both had attended Moscow Conservatory, where their classmates included Rachmaninov and Scriabin; what amazing piano stories they could tell.

Josef's death devastated Rosina, but she continued to concertize and teach until age 96. Van Cliburn, Misha Dichter, and John Williams were just a few of her outstanding students you may have heard of. I loved the Lhevinnes dearly. For years, when I visited New York to study music and attend concerts, I made it a point to spend time with them. They blessed my life with music, especially through the piano.

It was always my joy to provide financial support and encouragement to young musicians. After grandaddy Irwin died in 1910, I remember "Unk," (uncle Will, everyone else called him W. G.) took over our family home and expanded it greatly into its Edwardian style you see today. Not only did he provide the large, magnificent gardens modeled after ruins in Pompeii, but he also included several modern bathrooms, washers and dryers, a telephone room, elevator, and many more innovations. Daddy had expanded the mansion several times, too, and I can't remember if he or "Unk" designated one room as our music room—oh well, it makes no difference—music was a blessing for all. Uncle Will was such a successful entrepreneur—he could afford whatever he wanted to have—or what he wanted to give to others. He was incredibly generous. I tried to follow his example.

The music room in our family mansion wasn't just for me. My older sister, Nettie, also loved music thoroughly. We provided a variety of musical opportunities to our friends at Tabernacle Church and from the community. Wayne Berry was just a boy (the same age as my nephew, J. Irwin), and the two boys loved music-making as they grew up. Nettie and I started Clementine and J. Irwin on violin when they were very young. As they became adults, they were frequent performers in our family home music room: J. Irwin played violin, Clementine moved on to cello, and Wayne accompanied on my Steinway. What joy they brought me. All three were very talented.

Nevertheless, I could tell that Wayne Berry possessed exceptional musical talent. I had observed him in our music room, and as he served as organist at Tabernacle Church since he was fifteen years old. I witnessed firsthand, on a weekly basis, his musical gifts and development. I don't want to boast, but I did have extensive experience/exposure with exceptionally brilliant pianists. I knew talent when I heard it.

In addition to the Lhevinnes, I studied with Ernest Hutcheson, Australian pianist, who taught piano and became head of Juilliard. I studied with Hutcheson during many of my visits to New York. In Wayne Berry I saw the makings of a concert pianist, and I encouraged him to pursue that demanding career with all his heart and energy. Every time I had an opportunity, I urged Wayne and guided him toward a concert career. Of course, I dropped his name to those at Juilliard, and I was thrilled when Wayne studied with Bomar Cramer at Arthur Jordan School of Music in Indianapolis.

Cramer received the first scholarship in graduate piano study at Juilliard and went on to have exceptional performing opportunities, even as he headed the piano department at Arthur Jordan. Bomar Cramer helped prepare Wayne for his Juilliard audition. I was as pleased and proud as I could be. I could see Wayne becoming another Bomar Cramer. Naturally, Wayne was accepted for a graduate fellowship in piano at Juilliard, passing his audition with flying colors. Although he later changed musical direction away from the concert world, I always rejoiced in the part I played in Wayne Berry's early musical development.

I spent my life providing musical enrichment for others; such pursuit brought me joy and fulfillment. Izler Solomon and I worked diligently to see that Clowes Hall was constructed on the Butler University campus in Indianapolis, where it could be used for many types of musical performances. I rejoiced when the Metropolitan Opera included the venue for its productions. It was also my pleasure to help fund many projects at Indiana University. When I. U. School of Music established scholarships in my honor, I was very gratified. I was so blessed to have the financial resources of my family through the Irwin-Sweeney-Miller Foundation to undergird projects which brought music to many people at home, in Indiana, and throughout the world.

Chapter Thirteen: E. Wayne Berry Thrilled as New Organ Arrives

I was beside myself with excitement when the Aeolian-Skinner organ arrived at First Christian Church in 1942. Here was this unbelievable, jaw-dropping building that did not look like any church anyone had ever seen. It was over-the-top modern—stark and austere to many—and its setting among predominantly nineteenth-century buildings made it stand out even more. It took up an entire city block. There were also a 160-foot, freestanding tower and a reflecting pool. To say the facility was breath-taking is an understatement. It was monumental and stunning, but some people didn't like it. Admittedly, one had to get used to it, but it was impressive. And now it was time to install the organ. This was the project which had thrilled my soul during all the years it took to plan.

Our building committee worked diligently to construct this structure despite the war. We were so thankful metal for the organ pipes had been ordered and approved before war forced severe restrictions.[1] *The Diapason* ranked it as "one of the largest and most important" instruments completed "just previous to the war moratorium on organ construction."[2] It was right here in the Midwest, in Columbus, Indiana.

The organ arrived from Boston in three large vans. The console was unloaded and moved into the hall on the side of the new church sanctuary. Before it was installed, I used to take off the cover and try to imagine just how it would sound. The work of installation took about three months. I watched the progress with eagerness. The final voicing of the organ could not take place until all work and cleaning were finished in the sanctuary. The voicing engineer was a special person sent from the Boston factory for this delicate task. The voicer sat at the console with a partner in the organ. The voicer would play several keys, signal the change in volume of the pipe,[3] and this intricate process was repeated for each of the 4,720 pipes, until all pipes were voiced.[4] The entire installation process was incredibly detailed and time-consuming.

On October 22, 1946, a few years after the sanctuary organ was installed, the Indiana Chapter of the American Guild of Organists held one of its meetings at the church, and I performed a full program for about sixty guild members and many supportive attenders from the local community.

E. Wayne Berry was the organist and choir master at First Christian Church in Columbus. He helped design the 5,000-pipe organ for the church. He was also head of the music department at Cincinnati Bible College and Christian Seminary for 21 years. He passed away at the age of 94 in 2004. // Cincinnati Bible Seminary

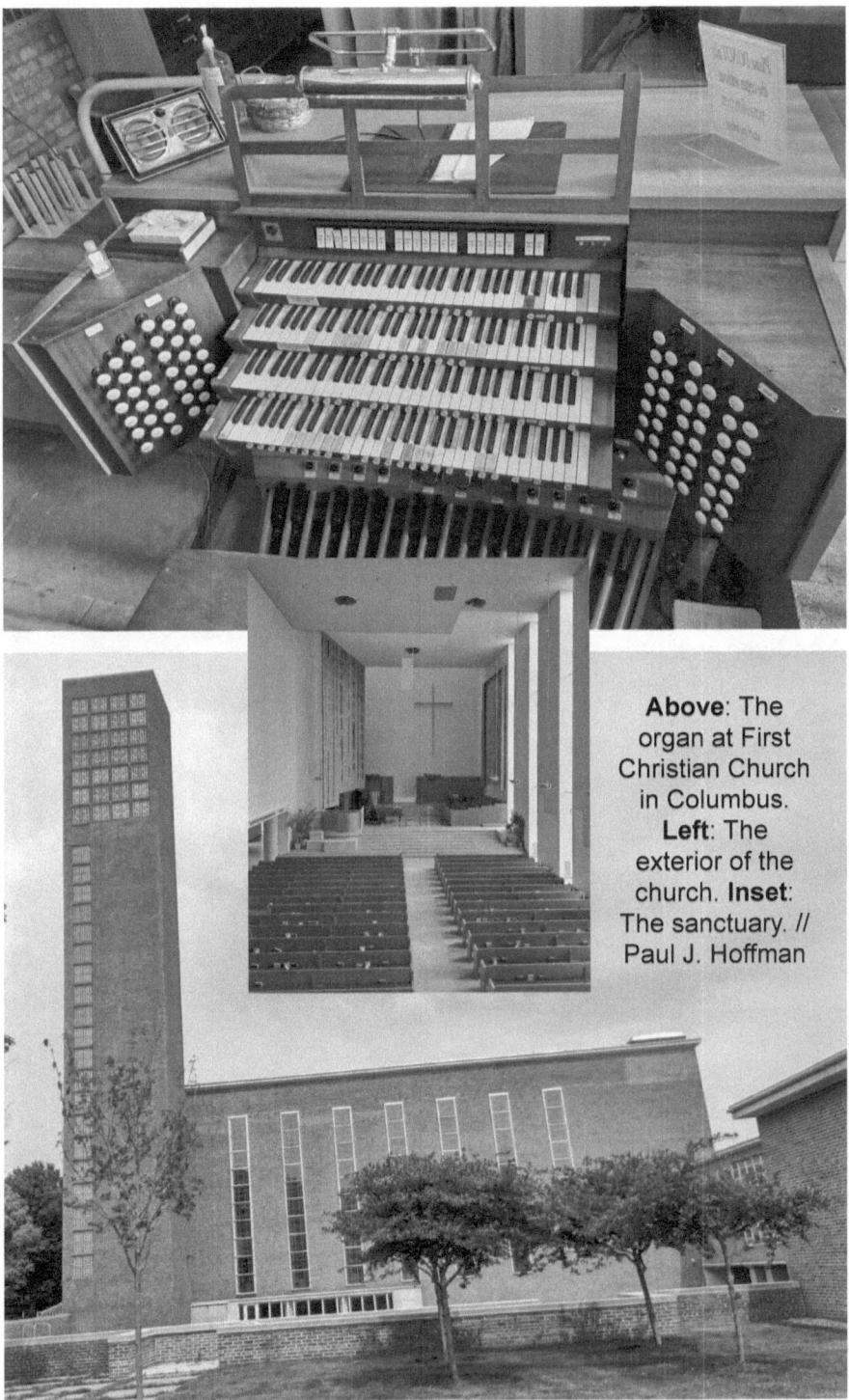

Above: The organ at First Christian Church in Columbus. **Left**: The exterior of the church. **Inset**: The sanctuary. // Paul J. Hoffman

It was an anxious, but thrilling moment for me as I presented the concert: J. S. Bach's Concerto in A minor, organ transcriptions of vocal music from J. S. Bach Cantatas 122 and 85, César Franck's Choral in E Minor, "Kyrie Eleison" and "Ave Maria" from *Cathedral Windows* by Sigfrid Karg-El-ert, and Sonata for Organ by Jaromir Weinberger.[5] Naturally, I chose a program to display the range of expression possible on the instrument.

Since the organ was the first of its kind to be heard in the Midwest, its brightness and volume elicited criticism from AGO members, and in time, we did make some tonal adjustments. But my initial anxiety was short-lived and, ultimate-ly, I was not unnerved. Before long, the guild regarded the organ as one of the "great instruments in the nation."[6] I felt vin-dicated, and I was proud of the ground-breaking design Carl Weinrich, G. Donald Harrison, and I had accomplished. Our deep gratitude went to Mrs. Nettie Miller for making this outstanding instrument possible. She paid for the organ—about $40,000.[7] (This would be more than $791,000 today.)[8]

Carl Weinrich, E. Wayne Berry's organ teacher and co-designer of First Chirstian Church's Aeolian-Skinner organ. // Westminster Records

I remember the organ aroused the curiosity of many famous organists, including Virgil Fox. He was a flamboyant organ virtuoso who played all his recitals from memory. In 1946, he became organist at the famous Riv-erside Church in New York City, where he later designed a huge Aeoli-an-Skinner organ for the congregation in 1948. (Riverside is where I had attended many memorable concerts during my graduate school days at Juilliard.) Fox appeared in a recital at Indiana University, about forty miles away in Bloomington, and wanted to play the organ in Columbus. One Thursday evening, as choir rehearsal was concluding, he arrived at the church, played some selections on the organ, and accompanied my wife, Frances, for some of her solos.[9] Those who stayed to listen heard an informal, free concert by Fox, who later earned the nickname the "Liberace of the organ." It was great fun—so exhilarating to be part of this impromptu recital.

For many years the Aeolian-Skinner Company serviced First Christian's organ through its Chicago office. Charles Englefrid usually made two trips each year, at Christmas and Easter, to tune and service the instrument.[10] I was blessed to have helped make this dream organ become reality; what a tremendous opportunity it had been to participate it its creation. The organ was "considered to be one of the nation's ten finest."[11] I also had the privilege of playing it for about twenty-five years for every type of occasion imaginable—what a blessing.

1. "Large Organ Opened in Unusual Ediface," *The Diapason*, 33:9 (August 1, 1942), p. 1.

2. Ibid.

3. Berry's Letter, p. 10.

4. pipeorgandatabase.org.

5. "E. Wayne Berry gives Recital," *The Evening Republican*, October 24, 1946.

6. Letter from E. Wayne Berry, August 27, 1988, p. 11.

7. Berry's Letter, p. 10.

8. amortization.org computation is made on the basis of 3.71% inflation from 1942 to 2024.

9. This incident was described in a telephone conversation with E. Wayne Berry on January 24, 1989.

10. Berry's Letter, p. 12.

11. Information from the Cincinnati Bible Seminary's printed program for 1965 Concert Choir Spring Tour.

SECTION V:

INSIGHTS

Chapter Fourteen: Women Equaled Men in Musical Projects

Nineteenth-century women played key roles in the musical development of Columbus. Jennie Bates was certainly ahead of her time and very accomplished; I wish we knew more about her. It is also hard to say how musical was Harriet Clementine Glanton Irwin, Joseph I. Irwin's wife. Little has been written about her, except that she was a dignified, strong woman who ran her home well and presented herself as a fitting mate for her exceptional husband.[1] By examining the Irwin-Sweeney-Miller women who followed as Harriet's descendants, it is not difficult to see that household leadership, business leadership, and, indeed, musical leadership qualities were combined and passed along from generation to generation.

By example—through nature, nurture, or both—women led, were creative and effective, and, at least as far as we know, not restricted in music of church and community. By the twentieth century, Louise Mason, Ida Edinburn, Jessie Kitchen, Eleanor Beauchamp, Myra Clippinger, Elise Kitzinger, Betty Frantz, Hazel Payne Crouch, Dorothy Poulton, and others assumed vital musical roles. Perhaps they learned from the example of earlier Irwin-Sweeney-Miller women.

Once Joseph Ireland Irwin's businesses thrived, he began to amass wealth quickly, and the family hired several servants. When sixteen-year-old Linnie married Z. T. Sweeney, she had never even combed her own hair.[2] Regardless of Harriet's specific gifts, she was considered a "born matriarch and ruled her part of the kingdom as rigidly as he [Joseph] ruled his."[3] What she demonstrated to her female descendants exemplified a high standard for forward-thinking and acting women, well beyond the cultural norms of mid-nineteenth-century Indiana.

Information below bears witness to this viewpoint; some points which appear earlier in this book are referenced again, simply for clarity and context. I note that Harriet Glanton Irwin's role was essentially managerial and administrative; thus, she provided a unique example for women in her family. She did not cook, clean, do laundry, or change diapers, but she saw that all of those tasks were done well by others. She was quite skilled in executive function, and so were her descendants.

Only two of Joseph and Harriet's six children survived to adulthood: William and Linnie. Their daughter, Linnie, two granddaughters, Nettie and Elsie, and one great-granddaughter, Clementine, made a formidable female quartet promoting music—in their home, church, community, state, and the world beyond. In the examples of Linnie and Nettie, musical influence was often behind the scenes but yielded very public results. Elsie, on the other hand, was not averse to participating where the musical action was—or where she thought it should be.

Despite the reality that Linnie was a wife at sixteen and mother at seventeen, she was able to delegate duties to several household servants, freeing her to work closely with Z. T. at church, or pursue business interests with her brother W. G. (brother and sister together owned half of Cummins Engine Company). Linnie prioritized piano study at the Central Indiana Conservatory of Music and probably studied with Professor William Bates, Jennie's husband. Regardless, she carefully directed music instruction for her two daughters, and her only son, Joseph, until his untimely death at age nineteen.

Of course, the entire family travelled freely, spending time at their summer home in Ontario, Canada, and taking extended trips to Europe. Linnie and Z. T. moved among highly-influential social circles in Europe, just as they did at home. Linnie and Elsie were presented at the court of King George V and Queen Mary in 1920.[4] Linnie oversaw Elsie's excellent piano accomplishments, and encouraged her grandchildren, Clementine and J. Irwin, while Nettie and aunt Elsie taught them violin. Linnie recalled her father's fine voice, Benjamin Hutchins' fine voice, and his never-waning emphasis on music education at church and in the town. True to their example, and perhaps as a tribute to her lost son's fine solo voice, she sponsored a children's choir at church for many years.

Linnie introduced all manner of culture, especially music, as her family traveled throughout the world; for approximately three years, she and Z. T. lived in Constantinople. She accompanied Elsie to Berlin for extended piano study with virtuoso Joseph Lhevinne. The two sailed from New York City in September 1913 on the *Imperator* and landed at Hamburg, they then proceeded to Berlin.[5] Ponder this possibility ... Elsie and her mother could have taken a fieldtrip to attend a production at Bayreuth's Festspielhaus during their 1913-1914 winter stay in Berlin. Richard Wagner had designed and opened his magnificent, ground-breaking opera house in 1876, and it was already world-famous when Linnie and Elsie spent extended time in Berlin.

They would have at least known about the Festspielhaus, so the seed may have been planted in Elsie's mind which bloomed much later in her life,

146

when she spear-headed the restoration of Wagner's unique opera house as a world center of music after World War II. Although Festspielhaus was not bombed, two-thirds of the city of Bayreuth was destroyed by American bombs, and Festspielhaus needed significant repair by the 1950s. In 1956 the Federal Republic of Germany awarded Elsie Sweeney the Officer's Cross, Order of Merit, for her significant leadership in restoring Wagner's Festspielhaus.[6] Elsie's reputation and music philanthropy were worldwide, but she directed all her musical projects from her Columbus, Indiana, home.

Elsie was a driving force in funding both the Indianapolis and Columbus symphony orchestras. After all, she had even performed as piano soloist in the second public performance of the Columbus Symphony in 1924. She established music scholarships and raised money for music facilities at Indiana University, and the university presented her numerous awards for her support. Together with Indianapolis Symphony conductor, Izler Solomon, Elsie strongly advocated—and aided fund-raising—for building Clowes Memorial Hall on the campus of Butler University in Indianapolis.[7]

Clowes Hall was a state-of-the-art, 2,000-seat performing venue which became the home of the Indianapolis Symphony in 1963 and remained so for more than twenty years. Piano may have been Elsie's first musical love, but opera was a close second. She suggested yearly performances of Wagner's *Parsifal* at I.U.[8] and helped bring the first Metropolitan Opera Productions of *La Boheme* and *La Traviata* to Clowes Hall in 1966 and 1967.[9]

__Author's Note:__ My first opera experiences were the Metropolitan Opera productions Elsie Sweeney brought to Clowes Hall when I was in high school. I had no idea who Elsie Sweeney was at that point, however the operas greatly impressed me. In addition to opera performances at Clowes, the hall was THE venue for every type of music production which came to Indianapolis from the time it opened in 1963.

Of course, Elsie was outspoken in her views, too. She criticized Tabernacle's organist for playing "The Shiek of Araby"[10] one Sunday morning. Paul Knarr was the church organist and also organist at Crump Theater. He sometimes recycled his theater repertoire for worship services, but Miss Elsie was not to be hoodwinked.

Nettie's Contributions

As mentioned in other chapters, Nettie, Elsie's older sister, strategized to hire E. Wayne Berry as First Christian's first full-time organist/choir director.[11] She succeeded, and by 1938 had persuaded her husband, Hugh—chairman of the board—to move this concept forward to its successful realization. She encouraged Berry to establish The Columbus A Cappella Choir in 1935, and her two children, Clementine and J. Irwin, were members of this elite ensemble which achieved an excellent statewide choral reputation. She financed Berry's advanced choral conducting with F. Melius and Olaf Christiansen, father/son conductors of the famed St. Olaf Choir in Wisconsin and with John Finley Williamson and his renowned Westminster Choir. She funded Berry's master's degree from Westminster Choir College, too.

It must not be forgotten that Nettie paid for First Christian's 81-rank Aeolian-Skinner organ in the congregation's 1942 ultra-modern structure. Her behind-the-scenes efforts yielded an innovative instrument designed by three experts (G. Donald Harrison, Carl Weinrich, and E. Wayne Berry), which was then handed over to world-class architect Eliel Saarinen to accommodate in his modern design. (See chapter eighteen.) Few realize the organ design preceded the sanctuary design.[12] Saarinen had to accommodate the previously designed organ while planning the sanctuary, but he seemed to take direction willingly from Nettie. She, like her sister, possessed incredible influence and resources.

Although Nettie was not a musical performer, Elsie was an accomplished pianist, as indicated by *The Evening Republican's* excellent review of her performance of Franz Liszt's *Un sospiro "A Sigh"* (the third of Liszt's beautiful, but "devilishly difficult" Transcendental Etudes in D-flat Major.)[13] She regularly invited E. Wayne Berry to play her Steinway in the family mansion's music room. It was the same room Berry often practiced piano, violin, and cello trios with Clementine and J. Irwin. No doubt, Nettie heard and enjoyed these private concerts, too. While Elsie was doing her best to guide Wayne toward a career as a concert pianist, Nettie seemed to bide her time, using equally strong influence and finding perfect opportunities to influence Wayne to pursue church music as his calling and career.

It could have been either Elsie or Nettie's influence that brought Metropolitan Opera diva Rose Bampton to Columbus for a performance at First Christian Church on March 14, 1943.[14] (I'm guessing Rose was a friend of Elsie's because of their common love of opera.) Bampton performed Rossini's "Inflammatus est", and Frances Berry graciously stepped aside from her usual rendition of the congregational favorite to let the world-famous guest soprano sing this powerful aria accompanied by the church choir. The choir—with many an outstanding soprano soloist through the decades—had treated the congregation to this thrilling selection from Rossini's *Stabat Mater* since it was first performed at the Christian Chapel in 1872. According to the printed program, Bampton also sang "I Know that My Redeemer Liveth," from Handel's *Messiah*.

Nettie's somewhat quieter, but nevertheless equally powerful, voice eventually prevailed for E. Wayne Berry's life's calling. It is noteworthy that after Berry was hired full-time at the church … after the impressive sanctuary and innovative organ became reality … after W. G. and Linnie established trust funds to finance building and organ maintenance, one final musical project remained for the creative Irwin-Sweeney-Miller women to pursue together.

__Author's note:__ Brother W. G. and sister Linnie died only seven weeks apart—W. G. Irwin on December 14, 1943, and Linnie Irwin Sweeney on February 2, 1944. Whereas W. G.'s death came as a shocking surprise, Linnie knew her days were numbered, and she urged everyone to move the church's building project along, so she could witness it all before she passed away. Only the final project mentioned below eluded Linnie's participation.

Elsie, Nettie, and Clementine collaborated with Wayne Berry to produce a hymnal, *Christian Hymns*, published by The Christian Foundation of Columbus in 1945. Berry may have spent great time and energy developing choral skills for the church and designing its distinctive pipe organ, but the hymnal project was perhaps the dearest to his heart. He believed strongly that congregational singing—not choral or organ music—was the very heart of church music, and he taught hymnology in his undergraduate and graduate courses. Therefore, he and the Irwin-Sweeney-Miller trio of ladies worked meticulously over this labor of love. Nettie and Elsie may have competed with each other in some of their earlier goals for a younger E. Wayne Berry, but in this hymnal effort they definitely worked together.

Furthermore, Clementine, only five years Berry's senior, focused on the love of hymns she shared with her fellow-music-maker from their youth. The family women used their expertise and money to compile a hymnal which served First Christian Church (and many Disciples of Christ congregations) for several decades; It also became the hymnal used in the Cincinnati Bible Seminary chapel services for decades. Nettie chose scripture texts to be used in connection with each hymn; Clementine assisted Berry in selecting hymns and editing them; and Elsie prepared indices and checked the proofs for printing. Berry acknowledged the assistance of Hugh Th. Miller, who also helped with editing and correcting proofs; Eliel Saarinen, who designed the book cover; Mrs. Wilbur Steinkamp, who assisted Elsie; and Edwin Errett, who edited responsive readings.[15] Again,

First Christian Church, stood out musically from a host of other congregations in the mid-twentieth century by publishing its own hymnal.

Clementine Miller Tangeman has been mentioned throughout this book, but there are some details which need to be highlighted. She married outstanding musician Robert Tangeman in 1951; unfortunately their marriage was cut short when Robert died suddenly in 1964 at age fifty-four.[16] He had been Harkness Professor of Sacred Music and Director of Graduate Studies for the School of Sacred Music at Union Theological Seminary.[17] Robert Tangeman had studied composition with Nadia Boulanger in Paris and taught music at Indiana University, where he and Clementine met.

Following his death, Clementine divided her time between New York City and Columbus. She continued generous support for various musical endeavors and was very involved in administration of the Girl Scouts. Clementine's service during World War II with the Red Cross in Italy no doubt paved the way for her future role with the Girl Scouts. Clementine also suggested the Sermon on the Mount as the theme for a specially woven tapestry which hangs above and behind the choir in First Christian's sanctuary.

__Author's Note:__ Clementine Miller Tangeman is the only member of the Irwin-Sweeney-Miller family I had the privilege of meeting during the 1980s, when I was doing research in Columbus. She greeted me at the door of the family mansion, and we had a brief, pleasant discussion in the room adjacent to the music room. She showed me a quilt created for her grandfather, Z. T. Sweeney; it contained a square with William and Jennie Bates' names—that was how I discovered Mrs. Bates' first name. I wish I had asked Clementine many more questions.

Dorothy F. Poulton was another talented and dedicated woman at First Christian Church. She sang in Wayne Berry's choral groups, was a capable soloist, and served faithfully for many years as teacher and co-superintendent for the Sunday School's beginner department. When she realized a book of songs suitable for children ages three through six could be a useful resource for her own congregation and many others, she compiled a collection, *Songs for Preschool Children*, published in 1946 by Standard Publishing. Poulton considered vocabulary limitations and musical capabilities of preschool children, as well as basic principles of Christian character in selecting more than 130 songs for her book.[18]

She chose songs by many composers, secured copyrights from several publishing companies, and wrote words and music for a number of songs included in the collection. Poulton grouped songs according to themes and devoted a large section to motion and finger play songs she considered suitable for use in nursery and beginner departments. Her foreword to the book echoes the spirit of a host of music educators who had been active in the church and community's music programs extending back to Benjamin Hutchins.

> *"A singing heart is a happy heart, and through music as a part of our life and worship, the life of a child can be made more complete. In the home and in the church we strive to teach children the basic principles of Christian character, and there is no better way than that of words which are within the understanding of the child, set in the frame of suitable music."*[19]

The women of First Christian Church were creative and productive in their use of music for special projects. Contributions by Linnie Irwin Sweeney, Nettie Irwin Sweeney Miller, Elsie Irwin Sweeney, and Clementine Miller Tangeman were particularly noteworthy. These last four women—representing three generations of the same family— created and supported wonderful, mind-boggling projects. Their energy, imaginations, and sense of innovation seemingly knew no bounds, and their influence and wealth provided musical blessings for future generations. They helped set a standard for modern women as movers and shakers—in business and especially in music—and their efforts were certainly not thwarted in church endeavors.

1.   William Marsh, "The Irwins and the Crumps," *I Discover Columbus* p. 151.

2.   Robert Earl Reeves, "A Biography of Z. T. Sweeney" (Master of Arts thesis, Butler University, 1959), p. 12.

3.   William Marsh, p. 151.

4.   www.Indianahistory.org.

5.   Rentschler, p. 19

6.   *The Evening Republican*, September 20, 1913.

7.   music.indiana.edu/giving/scholarships, p. 1.

8.   Clowes on Butler campus

9.   9 music.indiana.edu/giving/scholarships, p. 2.

10. bcplarchives.omeka.net. 032A-032D "Elsie Irwin Sweeney Newspaper Supplement."

11. Interview with Miss Mazie Denny on October 18, 1988.

12. Letter from Berry, p. 13.

13. Letter from Berry, p. 10.

14. The Republic, Saturday, Feb. 9, 1924

15. Printed program, March 14, 1943.

16. Letter from E. Wayne Berry, p. 13.

17. *The Columbus Herald*, "Robert Tangeman Dies in New York," October 2, 1964, p. 5.

18. www.nytimes.com.

19. Dorothy Poulton, Songs for Preschool Children: Standard Publishing Company, 1946, forward.

20. Ibid.

Chapter Fifteen: A World-Class Instrument in Columbus

During the mid-to-late 1930s, when Tabernacle Church of Christ was planning a new building, Nettie Irwin Sweeney Miller was also considering provisions for music in the proposed facility. She knew the congregation's music history very well through her grandfather, Joseph I. Irwin, who could have recalled to her the 1852 Christian Chapel, when the structure and its pipe organ were new. He also knew all details of the current organ at Tabernacle installed in 1879. (Perhaps grandfather told her about all the money he had given to maintain the church's organs, too. In 1892 the organ was rebuilt, and he paid for one third of the expense.)[1]

It now fell to Nettie to continue the legacy of exceptional organs for the congregation's third sanctuary. She accepted the challenge without hesitation, and the instrument resulting from her vision and influence was truly an innovative, monumental achievement.

Nettie had already provided the church's music program strong leadership by guiding Wayne Berry to his career in music ministry and providing financial resources for his graduate studies. When Berry studied organ in 1938 with Carl Weinrich at Westminster Choir College, he performed on a three manual Aeolian-Skinner instrument. Nettie proposed to Berry that he and Weinrich design an instrument "which would adequately serve the church."[2] She placed no financial limits on its design. The understatement of Nettie's directive cannot be glanced over; she was not advocating a budget-friendly instrument, and she certainly had the resources to give priority to the organ's design and capabilities.

Nettie's husband, Hugh Th., was an elder of the congregation, her uncle Will was chairman of the building committee, and her son, J. Irwin, was the primary influencer in pursuing modern architecture. The multi-faceted, massive undertaking was a family affair, and Nettie was protector and provider for the musical future of the church. Her long-lasting impact on the church was profound.

Author's Perspective: *Although E. Wayne Berry never clarified this point to me, I believe Nettie took it upon herself to take charge of the new organ*

First Christian Church building site, c. 1941. In the rear is old Tabernacle Christian Church. In the rear left is the Irwin-Sweeney-Miller mansion. The pipe organ had been designed before construction began.//Bartholomew County Historical Society

project for the new sanctuary. In other words, she needed no permission. The rest of her family seemed not to mind, and it also seems there was no opposition or approval required from any official group or board at church. Furthermore, there is every indication—from conversations with Professor Berry and his notes—that the entire family completely approved of Nettie's vision and all its ramifications for the rest of the entire building project. She didn't have to sell them on any aspect of her dream. I have no doubt regular discussions took place over meals at the mansion concerning the new building and organ. Free discussion of all types of issues and family business ventures was the norm in the multi-generational household.

In preparation for their design work, Berry and Weinrich visited several organs in the eastern United States. They determined, beginning with the sound of the Westminster chapel organ, that adjectives such as "clear, clean-cut, bright, and exciting" instead of "mild, heavy, and ponderous" would be qualities used to describe the sound they desired.[3] They found an organ sound which fit their description at St. Mark's Episcopal Church in Philadelphia.[4] Berry was so excited at the discovery that one afternoon he played almost his entire graduate recital on the instrument.

Organ Reform Movement in the United States

G. Donald Harrison (1889-1956) and Walter Holtkamp (1894-1962) were two chief spokesmen for the organ reform movement of the 1930s and early 1940s in the United States. Harrison had come from England in the 1920s to join the Skinner Organ Company in Boston. Holtkamp worked from Cleveland. The two men agreed that organ sound needed to be reformed, yet each worked quite independently and their approaches to organ building took quite different routes. Both organ innovators sought to produce a kind of all-purpose type of instrument, but Holtkamp was willing to work in a much smaller form than Harrison.[5]

One of the later twentieth-century experts in organ building, Thomas Wood of Indiana University, summarized Harrison's approach and its effect on the instrument he, Berry, and Weinrich designed. Thomas Wood wrote:

> *"Harrison's approach was to keep the basic Anglo-American organ design and expand it to the point of completing the ensemble divisions according to the principles of the Germanic classical instrument. His work evolved into what is now called the American classical organ. As always there must be a starting place. For a few years prior to First Christian's organ, Harrison had been promoting the idea that the fourth division should be a positif division and not a solo division since the stops of a solo division could be incorporated into the already existing enclosed divisions. I understand that at Christ's Church, Philadelphia, Harrison succeeded in preparing for a positif, but it was not installed initially. Indeed, the organ for Weinrich at Princeton contained a positif, but it is my understanding that the first instrument to be completed with this scheme was at First Christian, Columbus.*[6]

Thus, the resulting 1942 instrument was very innovative. It was designed in a rather unconventional way, too.

One day, Harrison, president of the Aeolian-Skinner Organ Company and good friend of Carl Weinrich, visited Westminster. That evening, Harrison, Weinrich, and Berry took a large sheet of paper, stretched it out on Weinrich's living room floor, and began to select the stops for divisions of the proposed organ. This is an amazing evening to contemplate; three experts in their fields were pipe-dreaming—pun intended—for the construction of their ideal pipe organ. Furthermore, they had every assurance the organ would be built; Nettie's vision was on the fast-track to reality, despite the nation's economic depression and impending world war.

Columbus, Indiana, may have seemed to be an unlikely location for this dream organ realization, but those closely involved had no doubts, whatsoever. The "imagineers" decided they would try to make the organ complete in the various divisions to the point of avoiding duplications such as I Diapasion, II Diapasion, III Diapasion as one manual.[7]

Unique Provisions and Construction

Once Harrison, Weinrich, and Berry completed their organ design, the contract was signed with the Aeolian-Skinner Company, even before architects Eliel and Eero Saarinen had been selected to design First Christian's new sanctuary.[8] Imagine conversations of W. G. Irwin, Nettie, Hugh Th. and J. Irwin Miller at the family home as they progressed with mind-boggling projects. J. Irwin pursued the contemporary design by the Saarinens, his mother, Nettie, advocated for the organ, and uncle W. G. Irwin chaired the building committee. Not only did Nettie pay for the organ, she also ensured that the Aeolian Skinner Company could specify the exact space and size requirements for the organ to Eliel Saarinen as he progressed with the building's design. The results of these unique circumstances are the relatively narrow pipe chambers and the open clear sound of the organ.[9]

In E. Wayne Berry's graduate classes at CBS, he often remarked that design, purchase, and placement of a church organ (pipe or electronic) reflected compromise. But obviously he was not bound by compromise in any aspect for organ design at First Christian Church—how singularly amazing. Nettie Sweeney Miller was Berry's benefactor, J. Irwin Miller was his lifelong musical friend, and W. G. Irwin was the passenger he often chauffeured to meetings in Indianapolis. Berry was smack-dab in the center of music, money, influence, and extraordinary achievements. Everyone was comfortable with their specific roles.

A Related Organ Story

Some years later (c. 1962-63), another multi-faceted organ story involved Berry and Mr. and Mrs. Edwin G. Crouch (also from First Christian in Columbus.) Edwin was former chief legal counsel at Cummins Engine Company, where J. Irwin Miller was company president; his wife, Hazel, was a musician who often worked with Berry. The Crouches gifted one of the early Allen electronic organ installations in Cincinnati to the Cincinnati Bible Seminary for the chapel, located at Price and Grand avenues in Price Hill. The three-manual instrument sounded amazing in the old chapel's wonderful acoustics; historic facade pipes were still displayed, thus many listeners never realized the organ was electronic and not a pipe organ. The Allen Company regarded its CBS installation as one of its finest.

From its installation until 1966, Wayne Berry performed each week on both organs—First Christian's distinctive pipe organ for Sunday worship services and CBS's distinctive electronic organ for chapel services and music department concerts. He served both institutions simultaneously.

Professor Berry was living on the cutting-edge of pipe organ and electronic organ invention and technology.

Other Special Organ Facts

Berry designed the First Christian organ console in a special way. Since he conducted the choir from the keyboard (as was his preference), he decided to omit the usual shelf at the lower edge of the stop panels and drop the draw knobs to a small distance above the positif keyboard. This arrangement resulted in greater convenience for both playing and conducting from the console.[10] Besides the sanctuary organ, the Aeolian-Skinner Company installed a three-rank unit organ in First Christian's chapel.

The congregation was fortunate that the contract for the organ was signed before any metal restrictions were enacted as a result of World War II.[11] *The Diapason* (August 1, 1942) commented that the organ ranked as "one of the largest and most important" instruments completed "just previous to the war moratorium on organ construction."[12] Nettie Miller provided approximately $40,000 for the construction of the four-manual, 81-rank instrument which included 72 speaking stops, 4,695 pipes, 61 harp bars, 25 chimes, together with 73 couplers and accessories.[13] The estimated reverberation time for organ sound in the sanctuary was about four seconds.[14] The AGO published a complete stop list which is still available online.

On October 25, 1942, E. Wayne Berry presented the first of three organ request concerts featuring favorite works chosen by the congregation.[15] The organ was brand-new. The first section of the program included Handel's "Largo" from *Xerxes* and "Pastoral Symphony" from *Messiah*, Franz Schubert's "Serenade," Richard Wagner's "O Thou Sublime Sweet Evening Star," J. S. Bach's "Joy of Man's Desiring," "See What His Love Can Do," and Toccata and Fugue in D Minor. Section two consisted of four congregational favorite hymns, which Berry, himself, arranged. The four hymns included "Faith of Our Fathers," "In the Garden," "The Old Rugged Cross," and "America, the Beautiful," (very appropriate since the nation was in the midst of World War II). Section three featured two settings of "Ave Maria," one by Schubert and one by Bach-Gounod, J. Brahms' Waltz in A flat, A. Liadow's "The Musical Snuff Box," and Liszt's "Liebestraum." Berry noted Schubert's "Ave Maria," and Bach's Toccata and Fugue in D Minor received the most votes from the congregation.

The favorites concerts highlight three revealing facts: 1) Congregational tastes were all over the music spectrum, 2) Berry was very wise to program three concerts of this nature, when the organ was brand-new and somewhat controversial, and 3) Some of the selections would probably still be favorites of today's church audiences. These three concerts solidified the congregation's ownership of their world-class instrument and helped them fall in love with it.

The Aeolian-Skinner Company regarded its installation at First Christian Church, Columbus, Indiana, as one of the finest in the nation. Numerous eminent organists have been drawn to the unique sanctuary and its distinctive organ. As recently as 2018, world-class organist and performer Diane Bish recorded a broadcast of her program *The Joy of Music* at First Christian.[16] She declared the organ to be outstanding—some eighty years after its original installation. Significant maintenance and improvements have been made to the instrument, funded by the trusts W. G. and his sister, Linnie, provided in their wills. Throughout the remainder of his life, even after leaving Columbus in 1966, E. Wayne Berry kept up with the organ, played it occasionally, and was apprised of work done and improvements made. He expressed approval of improvements made to the world-class instrument.

1. Deacons' Meeting Minutes, July 4, 1892, p. 4.

2. Letter from E. Wayne Berry, August 27, 1988, p. 9.

3. Ibid.

4. Ibid. p. 10.

5. Lawrence I. Phelps, *Short History of the Organ Revival* (St. Louis: Concordia Publishing House, 1967), p. 11.

6. Letter from Thomas Wood to Mr. Gaten Dismore, July 11, 1975, p. 2. Mr. Wood has overseen major renovations of the organ. He also taught organ construction at Indiana University School of Music.

7. Letter from Berry, p. 10.

8. Ibid.

9. Ibid.

10. Ibid.

11. "Large Organ Opened in Unusual Ediface," *The Diapason*, 33:9 (August 1, 1942), p. 1.

12. Ibid.

13. Berry's Letter, p. 10 and "The Organ," *A Century of Christian Progress 1852-1952*, Commemorating the 100th anniversary of the first permanent church building of The Christian Church, Columbus, Indiana, [n. p.].

14. Interview with Dan McKinley at First Christian Church, April 16, 1982.

15. printed program from Organ Request Concert, Sunday Evening, October 25, 1942.

16. www.thejoyofmusic.org 9208 A Musical Visit to Columbus, Indiana.

Chapter Sixteen: Symbiotic Relationships—Mostly

Snapshot memories and random facts combine to provide fascinating connections between Clessie Cummins, E. Wayne Berry, and the family of generous benefactors who invested in both creative men. Clessie Cummins and W. G. Irwin began their entwined stories in the Irwin family garage when Clessie was just a teenager. J. Irwin Miller's participation and influence came into play later, when he was hired at Cummins Engine Company in 1934. Although Wayne Berry's story was directly influenced by Irwin-Sweeney-Miller women, he and W. G. shared many connections, and he became a figure of some importance to Clessie's boat-building project. J. Irwin Miller's musical involvement with E. Wayne Berry, through singing and playing violin since childhood at First Christian, grew naturally as both men matured; such details are spelled-out in chapter seven.

W. G. Irwin never drove a car; he hired Clessie Cummins (1888-1968), whose formal education ended at age sixteen, as family chauffeur and mechanic in 1908.[1] Cummins tinkered with all kinds of machines, especially engines, in the Irwin-Sweeney-Miller garage, eventually improving a diesel engine design, which W. G. deemed worthy of very significant financial backing. Wayne Berry tinkered with engines, too. Many years later (1966-1968) he rode a motorcycle between his Cincinnati home and the CBS campus. (The author recalls witnessing his professor/organist/pianist's bandaged hand following some sort of "fixing" accident.)

Berry helped Clessie build a boat—a big boat. There is a photo showing Berry on his back, working beneath the thirty-six-foot *Big Dipper*, as Clessie named it. Several friends came to Clessie's farm west of Columbus to help construct his *Big Dipper* beginning in the summer of 1940. By 1944 Clessie launched the "*Big Dipper* on the Ohio River at Madison, Indiana, and set sail for Fort Meyers Beach, Florida.[2] Berry's toddler daughter Gyneth and Clessie's youngest son, Lyle, appear in the photo, playing while Berry glued many plugs to cover planking screws on the underside of the craft. The photo presents a visual account of friends helping each other, having fun, and realizing their dreams. People said Clessie never knew a stranger; he was not only an inventor, but an effective, affable salesman, too.

W. G. took the lead encouraging Clessie Cummins' inventions and gave him incredibly generous financial backing—often in ten-thousand-dollar increments— for what started out as Cummins Engine Company in 1919–a company which took until 1937 to make a profit. Brother and sister, W. G. and Linnie, were the engine company's faithful supporters through extremely lean years. Their investments eventually totaled nearly $2 million.[3] As for the company, it grew into Cummins Diesel, a multi-billion-dollar Fortune 500 company decades later, under J. Irwin Miller's effective leadership. J. Irwin eventually led Cummins Diesel to worldwide recognition and success.

In 1932 Clessie chauffeured W. G. on a 5,000-mile road trip through Europe and England, driving a Duesenberg powered by Clessie's diesel engine (J. Irwin, a student at Oxford, accompanied them for part of the trip). The Duesenberg was shipped to Europe for the grand tour. W. G. introduced Clessie to a world of culture he had never known. At many stops, regardless of the country or language barrier, Clessie communicated the marvels of his engine to anyone who would try to listen and comprehend. (Incidentally, this is the car that set a diesel speed record at Daytona Beach, Fla., in 1931. It was also the car that completed the 1931 Indianapolis 500 without making any pit stops.). Over a period of fifty years Clessie Cummins secured thirty-three US patents for his inventions. He was always improving his products.

W. G. Irwin and Hugh Th. Miller—husband of Nettie, W. G.'s niece—had long, strong ties with Butler University, and their family had supplied significant financial support to the institution for most of a century. Miller was quite a scholar, having studied at the Sorbonne in Paris, and served on Butler's faculty as Spanish and history professor; both he and W. G. were directors. W. G. was also president of the Butler University Foundation. These two family members/businessmen had plenty of clout, and they used it successfully to encourage the university to hire E. Wayne Berry as special lecturer in church music.

W. G. became president of Indiana National Bank in 1942 and enlisted Berry to chauffeur him for weekly bank meetings in downtown Indianapolis—Clessie had become much too busy inventing and publicizing his innovations to continue as W. G.'s chauffeur. Combined influence by W. G. and Hugh Th. ensured that Berry's teaching schedule at Butler coincided with W. G.'s bank meetings. Their efforts worked out perfectly, and everyone's weekly responsibilities were coordinated. It's amazing how "connected" people can use their influence for the good of others.

By late 1943, Wayne Berry was somewhat of an informal chauffeur successor to Clessie Cummins. Berry and W. G. had great conversations while traveling back and forth between Columbus and Indianapolis each week. Their range of subjects included the war, government purchases from

Cummins, news from J. Irwin serving in the Navy, and other common interests—church, philanthropy, engines, music, business, and growing all manner of plants, flowers, and trees. Thirty years earlier W. G. had established large, impressive sunken gardens adjacent to the family mansion; the gardens were inspired by ruins he had seen in Pompeii. Berry had just purchased Fruitland, a 200-acre orchard of approximately 5,000 apple and plum trees.

It was W. G. Irwin and his sister, Linnie Irwin Sweeney, who created trusts to fund future maintenance of First Christian Church's one-year-old, world-famous structure and world-class organ.

Clessie and W.G. had always had much to talk about, too. They valued and loved each other as dear friends, but also disagreed concerning matters at the engine company. They spoke honestly and firmly to one another, but occasionally in anger. Sometimes J. Irwin had to navigate carefully between both men who were dear to him. Clessie's genius was focused on inventions, while W. G.'s gifts were divided among many demanding projects which involved maintaining, growing, and overseeing an array of family businesses. Clessie was aware of W. G.'s heart condition, too, and attempted to communicate carefully with his mentor. However, he wrote a letter on December 13, 1943, expressing extreme displeasure with W. G. and the engine company. W. G. received the letter the next morning and read it; it caught him completely off-guard and really upset him.

That same morning, December 14, 1943, following regular routine matters in Columbus and a fifty-mile trip to Indianapolis, Nettie, rather than Clessie or Wayne, as one might expect, drove her uncle to his downtown Indianapolis office. She, no doubt, used their time together to calm his nerves. It seemed peace had been restored when they arrived at Indiana National Bank. Very soon, however, W. G. complained of being warm and short-of-breath. By 11:05 am he was pronounced dead, having suffered a massive heart attack.[4]

W. G. Irwin's death was a tremendous shock to everyone—not just in Columbus and Indianapolis, but throughout the banking, investing, business, and Christian worlds of America (he had also been a significant voice on the board of Standard Publishing in Cincinnati). Wherever he served, he was a powerful influence for good. People from all walks of life knew and respected this quiet (almost timid), wealthy, influential, yet down-to-earth multi-millionaire man of faith, who never married. What a sudden jolt of reality and reflection befell everyone that day—especially J. Irwin Miller on a U. S. Navy ship in the Pacific,

and long-time friends and one-time chauffeurs, Clessie Cummins and
E. Wayne Berry.

1.   p. 27, Cummins, C. Lyle, Jr., *The Diesel Odyssey of Clessie Cummins*. Austin, Texas: Octane Press, Edition 2.0, 2023, p. 27.

2.   Ibid. p. 307.

3.   Ibid. p. 334.

4.   *The Evening Republican*, Tuesday, December 14, 1943, p. 2.

Chapter Seventeen: Church Music Philosophy and Standards

At the time *A Suggested Outline for a Musical Program for This Church* was written, First Christian Church's music program would have been the foremost example of local church music ministry among Restoration Movement congregations in the United States. However, at the same time, First Christian's music program would have more than held its own in comparison with *any* congregation of more than a thousand members across the denominational world in the USA. Comparisons with large congregations in much larger cities than Columbus would have provided similar findings; yet, once again, Columbus' musical context was amazing for its size and the times.

Times were different before the advent of the current mega-church. Traditional and contemporary references to music and worship styles were yet to evolve. And so, we open the pages and take another peek into history, but we contemplate a mid-twentieth-century view much closer to present-day reality.

The information below was compiled and presented by J. Irwin Miller, CEO of Cummins Engine Company, the corporation he led to become a Fortune 500 company, and Cummins still appears on the Fortune 500 list today—long after Miller's death. However, this document represents a unique appraisal combining perspectives of a wealthy business executive with more than one hundred years of family history and unique association with the congregation's music program. It fascinates me that J. Irwin's formal education was not in business, rather he majored in the classics. He had no problem transitioning from a classical education to a very successful business executive. Basically, he combined both worlds in his life.

J. Irwin Miller compiled the document below less than two months after his father's death on May 26, 1947. This point of reference is important in interpreting J. Irwin's perspective. His father, Hugh Th. Miller, excelled in many fields and was a very influential leader. He was artistic, philosophical, and practical in his approach to life and management of various concerns. I'm sure J. Irwin had processed his father's ideas (his mother Nettie's and aunt Elsie's, too), making them his own, and presenting them in his voice.

Although today's church musicians will use very different terminology, careful study of the points emphasized, should help readers realize that

Miller was weaving business ideas with his music philosophy, standards, and analysis. Although some of his points speak only to his time, many can be transferred to today's congregations, despite differences in musical style from the 1940s.

J. Irwin and E. Wayne Berry performed music together beginning as children, and thus, I'm sure they also discussed music. Their tastes and appreciation were quite similar. J. Irwin indicated he conferred with E. Wayne, and, therefore, Berry's voice is woven into the standards set forth. Such principles and ideas would have been found in Berry's teaching during more than two decades as special lecturer in church music at Butler University and more than two decades as department chair at Cincinnati Bible Seminary. I know Berry's music philosophy principles and standards were part of his graduate class, Ministry of Music—because I took the class.

Although we must update terminology, expanding "hymns" to include worship songs and praise choruses; realize many churches have praise bands instead of (or, in addition to) organists; recognize that music education programming has been essentially eliminated in many churches; and acknowledge all complexities technology has brought, it is worth gleaning truths which transcend some eighty years for musicians, worship leaders, and congregations … perhaps businessmen, too.

A Suggested Outline for a Musical Program for This Church

J. Irwin Miller

July 1947

The Purpose of the Musical Program of this church:

To make Christianity more effective in the lives of the persons who attend this church.

How is its purpose achieved?

1. Through the worship services:

a. Acts to unite the whole service and emphasize its selected theme.

b. Offers, through hymn-singing, a means for the congregation to participate actively in the worship service.

c. Affords, through selected appropriate anthems and solos, dramatic presentations of the great Christian texts and themes.

d. Works to contribute to the whole worship service a feeling of the presence of God.

2. Through the church's social activities:

a. Provides a constant source of acceptable and attractive entertainment.

3. Through the activities of the church's musical groups:

a. Offers to musical individuals a means of serving their church.

b. Affords additional opportunity for groups of church members to engage in common Christian work.

c. Offer to all an opportunity to become acquainted with and/or take part in one of the greatest expressions of religious faith, i.e., religious music.

4. Through the quality of the music presented:

a. It takes first-class means to product first-class results.

What persons execute this program, and what part does each play?

1. The Director of Music:

Duties: To select, prepare, execute, and evaluate.

a. Selection:

1. Have weekly conference with minister to have theme, subject or text for the services of the week.

2. Select appropriate and timely music and hymns for services.

3. Organize and prepare for printing program of services.

4. Examine regularly new material to broaden the work of the department of music and make its work more effective.

5. Collect and study other church bulletins with idea of improving our services.

6. Have full knowledge of present church music library and use it to fullest extent and best advantage.

b. Preparation:

1. Develop congregational singing—by calling attention of congregation to meaning of hymns and reason for selection; by general encouragement to sing; by organizing hymn services and hymn festivals; by using choirs, not singing service, in balcony (or any effective location) to sing with congregation; by using hymn stories; by hymn discussions and demonstrations at fellowship dinners, or at other social affairs of the church; gospel hymns, by general display of enthusiasm for hymns, by planned and systematic program of hymn singing throughout Sunday School.

2. Development of Choirs—Children's Choir, High School Choir, Church choir, and other groups which are considered necessary. Each choir must rehearse once a week with other rehearsals as necessary. Choir loft (seats 48 adults) should be used as goal for membership, but emphasis should be placed on quality in Church Choir. In Children's Choir and High School Choir numbers are very important—singing to be simple in difficulty to obtain good quality, though large numbers. Choirs to be used in regular services and at Christmas and Easter. Special services of music must be arranged to continue customs of church. Full facilities of church's sound system should be understood and used with choirs and organ.

3. Development of small groups and individual performers. Have small groups available to church for social activities, such as solos, duets, quartets, etc. Some individual instruction should be given to those who can benefit most from it. Instrumental instruction, especially piano and organ, should be given to make more effective the playing of hymns in Sunday School and to provide for substitute organists in the church program.

4. Organ practice. Regular organ practice and development of large organ repertory and preparation of organ recitals must be part of the work.

5. Systematic and regular planning for all rehearsals of choral groups must be practices.

c. Execution:

1. Play organ and conduct all services of the church.

2. Unify organ playing and details of services, such as unity of service by theme, by careful selection of key, by timing various parts of service according to effect, traffic, etc.

3. Playing of special services, such as weddings, funerals, etc.

4. Performing services of music, including the greatest expressions of praise of God in large musical works.

5. Carrying out advertising program connected with all special programs of the musical department of the church.

6. Worship services of organ music … organ recitals at intervals throughout the year.

7. Directing youth choirs in services and on other occasions.

d. Evaluation:

1. Should continually observe and study the effectiveness of each part of the musical program as executed.

2. Should continually endeavor to improve the effectiveness of each part of the musical program.

2. The Minister

a. Should have interest in and develop acquaintance with the great Christian musical literature.

b. Should work closely with the Director of the Music to build and maintain effective worship services.

c. Should actively support and encourage each of the church's musical groups.

d. Should, at regular intervals, instruct the congregation how to participate in and benefit from each part of the worship services.

e. Should encourage the congregation, through personal example, in effective and understanding singing of hymns.

What are the qualifications desired of a director of music to enable him to execute his part of this program?

1. Genuine love for and interest in the principles of the Christian Church.

2. Genuine interest in the possibilities of using music to unite Christians.

3. Real spirit of cooperation which will make possible:

a. The practical application of Christian unity through music with other churches.

b. Constructive work with many people.

c. The appreciation of the musical ability of others.

4. Natural ability and at least minimum experience required to begin building a long-time worship and music program for the church.

5. Musicianship. This important requirement attempts to define that subtle quality called "talent," but this quality gives life, movement, and vitality to music.

6. Technical Ability. Formal academic training and sufficient practice to perform the mechanical aspects of conducting and playing the organ and piano.

7. Should have extensive organ repertory. Not only is it important to be able to play organ, but the director of Music should have played organ music from all historical periods. He should understand the problems of organ registration in all periods. He should know how to register and play this type of organ ... that is, the modern ensemble type of instrument. He should be enthusiastic about this organ and should not limit the instrument by trying to play it like the so-called standard organ.

8. He should own an adequate collection of organ music and should be prepared to expand it. The present collection used is valued at about $1,000. The church has no collection of organ music.

9. He should have an extensive knowledge of choral literature. This must be wide enough to include at least the large choral works sung by the present Church Choir and should be far beyond this in order to lead the choirs on a program of progressive attainment.

10. He should understand problems of small town church programs. Must have interest in and respect for those of inferior vocal and instrumental attainment.

11. He must know how to use average voices to form a choir.

12. He must have a knowledge of voice training of adult singers.

13. He must have a knowledge of voice training of children.

14. He should develop an extensive knowledge of our hymnbook and all phases of hymnology to choose music for services and to have a general background for choices of worship.

15. He must be able to judge the merit of hymns, both text and tune.

16. He should know how to locate and be constantly interested in locating new material.

17. He should have knowledge and experience in program building.

18. He must have willingness to submerge his own personality into the task of creating church worship experiences.

19. He must believe in and practice and use the working principle ... that individual personalities should not be featured in public worship and that praise of God and the creation of an avenue or instrument for praise and the bringing of man closer to God is the high task of the director of music, and thus ... make Christianity more effective in the lives of those who attend this church.

—GARDEN PARTY—
Wednesday, July 2, 1952
7:30 P. M.

Song Service

Devotions "Lanterns" -- Mrs. Edgar Spies

Offering

THROUGH THE YEARS --- Vincent Youmans
AT DAWNING --- Chas. Wakefield Cadman
BECAUSE --- Guy d'Hardelot

Mrs. E. Wayne Berry, soprano
Mrs. Edwin G. Crouch, contralto

SONATA IN E MAJOR --- J. S Bach
    Adagio
        Allegro
            Adagio, ma non tanto
                Allegro
                    J. Irwin Miller, violinist
                    E. Wayne Berry, pianist

A BROWN BIRD SINGING --- Haydn Wood
GYPSY LOVE SONG -- Victor Herbert
BY THE BEND OF THE RIVER ---------------------------------- Clara Edwards
WILL YOU REMEMBER (Sweethearts) ------------------------- Sigmund Romberg

Mrs. Berry and Mrs. Crouch

Program for a garden party, held on July 2, 1952, sponsored by the Women's Council of First Christian Church.Following the church's centennial celebrations in 1952, this garden party performance was probably one of the last times E. Wayne and J. Irwin played music together.

SECTION VI:

FINALE

Chapter Eighteen: A Very Human Sacrifice of Praise

I returned to First Christian Church in 1984, after I had become music department chair at CBS and conductor of concert choir. (Professor Berry held both these positions, and I aspired to both of them from the time I was fifteen.) Concert choir was on spring tour, and I was thrilled to perform at the church where so many intriguing stories had originated, and so much amazing music had been performed and heard. What transpired has been sealed in my memory for decades, and it has taken me time to process fully.

The former alumni director at CBS, Harold Armstrong, had become senior minister at First Christian, and we were friends. Upon arrival, Harold said, "We want the entire choir to rehearse and change into their tuxedos and dresses before we serve them dinner tonight. The meal will be served at … " I agreed, but also knew the choir would much rather rehearse, eat, and then change clothes; nevertheless, I complied with the request. I had to do a little persuading and remind the choir we must be polite guests.

We were rehearsing in the sanctuary, and Dan McKinley—the music minister and organist at the time—assisted us. My excellent student accompanist, Ken, studied both piano and organ, and I asked Dan if Ken could play the magnificent organ and accompany John Ireland's *Greater Love Hath No Man*. I wanted Ken to have the thrill of playing the organ. Dan complied but cautioned this might be a challenge for a student organist with little practice time. However, Dan helped Ken, and rehearsal went well. I, too, was thrilled that the choir, Ken, and I would be able to experience the glorious sound of such an instrument in concert. I wanted the choir to experience what Professor Berry had helped design, too. Hearts raced as we rehearsed; everyone was excited. We concluded rehearsal in high spirits, and I dismissed everyone to change for dinner.

When we arrived at dinner, we were seated at round tables with tablecloths, china, and silverware. There were table decorations, lights were dimmed, and beautiful piano music was being played by Bernie Blankenship, another staff member. It was delightful and very special. We suddenly understood why we had been asked to change before dinner; it was as if we were at prom. We were served at our tables and treated like royal guests. How very thoughtful and welcoming. We felt loved. What a fun night we were having.

The choir really enjoyed being pampered during the meal, and they were primed to give their all in the concert to follow. They sang extremely well, and I was reveling in the glorious experience. We performed from the front steps of the stage, facing the audience, and Ken had to use a mirror on the organ console to see my conducting when it came time for him to play the one selection.

I knew "Greater Love Hath No Man" was familiar to the congregation; it had been part of First Christian's choir repertoire for decades. As we sang the anthem, all went well through the glorious full choir, full organ sound "that ye should show forth the praises of Him who has called you out of darkness, out of darkness— into his marvelous light!" Following a mighty, majestic organ measure, the choir entered, pianissimo, a cappella for, "I beseech you, therefore, by the mercies of God that you present your bodies a living sacrifice, holy, acceptable unto God, which is your reasonable service." On the second syllable of "be-seech" what should have been a very soft organ entrance was in reality an ear-splitting, loud mass of wrong notes. Ken had hit the wrong piston to change registration, and it completely flustered him—momentarily—but, of course, it seemed like an eternity. In the mirror Ken's face appeared scarlet, the choir was in shock, wide-eyed, and some physically jerked because they were so startled. I was dumb-founded and kept going, perspiring as if I were in a sauna, but it took until "which is your reasonable service" to regain composure, as well as right notes, accompaniment, registration, and volume. Whew! This was an experience never to be wished on anyone.

Immediately, I felt sorry for Ken—for the choir—for the audience—for myself—for GOD! In this glorious space, with this magnificent organ, honoring the legacy of Professor E. Wayne Berry, had we let everyone down? We had just sung "acceptable unto God" and given catastrophic musical commentary to those convicting words. My mind was a jumble, but I had to regroup and conduct the remainder of the concert. Thankfully, we all got back on track quickly … Praise God for such blessings.

In time, we were able to recall the horrible faux pas light-heartedly. Ken recovered his composure, and we loved him for being so vulnerable—besides, rehearsal had gone well. Everything had been prepared for a very special evening for us and for the congregation. Careful reflection told me the glorious space and magnificent organ had surely witnessed other disasters and near-disasters—if not in performance (and I doubt that is true)—then surely in rehearsal. Seeking comfort for all of us as flawed musicians, I recalled my wife's regular perspective, "No one performs perfectly, except Jesus."

What seemed such a failing on my part, as an overly-ambitious leader who was pushing too hard, eventually led me to realize all the previous decades of striving for excellence which had taken place—to create this space and create music *in* this space—represented the striving of men and women seeking to present worthy "reasonable service." Seasoned musicians (even extremely stubborn ones) learn eventually, when something completely out of everyone's control happens, chalk-it-up to being human, and go on. Reasonable service does NOT mean perfect service. In my writing and research, I knew this congregation had been striving to push the envelope of musical achievement for more than one hundred and twenty years. I, too, was endeavoring to create an excellence-expanding insight for my student musicians. Therefore, whoever didn't understand just needed to live longer and realize "living sacrifices" are human beings. God made us, and He understands us. Furthermore, we were very thankful to Him and to First Christian Church in Columbus. Amen.

Bibliography

Books

Bartholomew County Historical Society. *History of Bartholomew County, Indiana,1888, Vol. I*; rpt. Columbus, Indiana: Avery Press, 1976.

Atlas of Bartholomew County, Indiana,1879, Evansville, Indiana: J. H. Beers & Co., 1879.

Cummins, Jr., C. Lyle, *The Diesel Odyssey of Clessie Cummins*. Austin Texas: Octane Press, 2023.

Ellinwood, Leonard. *The History of American Church Music*. New York: Morehouse-Gotham Co., 1953.

Errett, Isaac. *Our Position*. Cincinnati, Ohio: Standard Publishing, 1870.

Fish, Henry R. *Illustrated Columbus, Indiana, 1915*. No publishing information, n. d.

Hitchcock, H. Wiley. *Music in the United States: A Historical Introduction*, 2nd Edition. Englewood Cliffs, New Jersey: 1974.

Marsh, William E. *I Discover Columbus*. Oklahoma City: Semco Color Press, 1956.

Marter, Joan et al. *Design in America, the Cranbrook Vision 1925-1950*. New York: Harry N. Abrams, Inc., 1983.

Mote, Patricia M. *Images of America: Columbus*. Charleston, South Carolina: Arcadia Publishing, Co. 2005.

McAllister, Lester G. *Z. T. Sweeney, Preacher and Peacemaker*. St. Louis: Christian Board of Education. 1968.

March, James Deforest. *Christians Only*. Cincinnati, Ohio: Standard Publishing, 1962.

Phelps, Lawrence I. *Short History of the Organ Revival*. St. Louis: Concordia Publishing House, 1967.

Rentschler, Charles E. Mitchell. *The Cathedral Builder: A Biography of J. Irwin Miller*. Bloomington, Indiana: AuthorHouse, 2014.

Theses and Dissertations

Cartwright, Byron James. *A History of the Music Ministry of First Christian Church, Columbus, Indiana.* D. M. A. dissertation, The Southern Baptist Theological Seminary, 1989.

Gemmeke, Richard Harold. *W. G. Irwin and Hugh Thomas Miller: A Study in Free Enterprise in Indiana.* Ph.D. dissertation, Indiana University, 1955.

Rightmyer, James. *A Documentary History of the Music Program of Second Presbyterian Church, Louisville, Kentucky, 1830-1980.* D. M. A. dissertation, The Southern Baptist Theological Seminary, 1980.

Reeves, Robert Earl. *A Biography of Z. T. Sweeney.* Master of Arts thesis, Butler University, 1959.

Westberry, Gilbert Foster. *A History of the Music Ministry of the First Baptist Church of Jeffersontown, Kentucky from 1845 to the Present.* D. M. A. dissertation, The Southern Baptist Theological Seminary. 1971.

Articles from Multivolume Works and Periodicals

"Businesses Rebuild an Indiana Town." *Fortune Magazine*, 50:1 (July 1954), 92.

Errett, Edwin. "The Building Committee Writes the Architect." *Christian Standard.* 67:21 (May 23, 1942), 4.

Jeffery, David. "A Most Uncommon Town Columbus." *National Geographic.* (September 1978), 383.

"Large Organ Opened in Unusual Edifice." *Diapason.* 33:9 (August1, 1942), 1.

Robinson, Ray. "John Finley Williamson: His Contribution to Choral Music." *The Choral Journal*, (September 1981), 5.

Stopp, Jacklin Bolton. "A. N. Johnson, Out of Oblivion." *American Music*, 3:2 (Summer 1985), 163.

"Tabernacle Church of Christ Dedication." *Christian Standard*, (February 15, 1879), 52.

Course Syllabus

North, James B. "History of the Restoration Movement." Course Syllabus, Cincinnati Christian Seminary, 1981.

Interviews with Author

Armstrong, Harold. September 8, 1988.

Cook, Marie. September 18, 1982.

Denny, Mazie. April 18, 1982, and October 18, 1988.

Dismore, Margaret. August 30, October 18, 1988, January 17-18, 1989.

Dismore, Margaret. Personal Notes on Sam Chizmar, January 17, 1989.

Keaton, Georgiana. April 7, 1982.

McKinley, Daniel. April 16, 1982.

Schumacher, Josephine Hutchins (daughter of Benjamin M. Hutchins). August 30, 1988.

Smith, C. Lee. April 16, 1982.

Tangeman, Clementine Miller. June 30, 1989.

Letters to Author

Berry, E. Wayne. August 27, 1988 and January 23, 1989.

Sherwood Conservatory of Music. October 28, 1988.

Tangeman, Clementine Miller. August 21, 1988.

Questionnaires from Author

Bohn, Martin. August 1988.

Chandler, Jeanne Bray. September 1988.

Denny, Mazie. August 1988.

Dismore, Margaret. September 1988,

Mattox, Frank. August. 1988.

Smitley, Vernon. (including dossier). August 1988.

Telephone Conversations with Author

Berry, E. Wayne. January 24, 1989; September 6, 1988.

Dismore, Margaret. February 11, 1989.

McKinley, Daniel. August 8, 1989.

Sims, Earl. February 16, 1989.

Spinks, Greg. January 4, 1989.

Stopp, Jacklin Bolton. July 31, 1988.

Wymore, Leonard. September 19, 1989.

Bartholomew County Historical Society

Arnold, Laura Fawcett. "Singing School." *Ye Olden Time* May 1897; rpt. Columbus, Indiana: *Bartholomew County Historical Society's Scrap Book No. 10–#339*, 1980, 108.

Central Indiana Conservatory of Music files.

Columbus Symphony Orchestra files.

Indiana Music Teachers' Association Official Program, Twenty-Third Meeting at Columbus, Indiana. June 26-29, 1900.

Irwin, Joseph I. files.

Irwin, W. G. files.

Kitzinger, G. Chester. File of personal notes.

Mason, Arthur. files

Miller, Hugh Th. files.

Sweeney, Elsie. files.

Sweeney, Z. T. files.

Irwin Management

Irwin-Sweeney-Miller files.

Registry of Members of the Christian Chapel, Columbus, Indiana, Joseph I. Irwin, clerk. [n. d., n. p.].

First Christian Church

Aeolian-Skinner Pipe Organ Information Sheet and Notes compiled by Thomas Wood, Jun 15, 1983.

Berry, E. Wayne, Clementine Miller Tangeman, and Edwin Errett. *Christian Hymns*. Columbus, Indiana: The Christian Foundation, 1945.

Berry, E. Wayne. Employment Agreements with Tabernacle Church of Christ.

Board Meeting Minutes. July 1892-January 3, 1894.

Program for Centennial Services 1852-1952.

A Century of Christian Progress 1852-1952, Commemorating the 100th Anniversary of the first permanent church building of The Christian Church, Columbus, Indiana, 1952.

"Chancel Choir Annuals," 1964-65 and 1965-66.

Deacons' Meeting Minutes. December 3, 1888 through 1929.

Dedication Program, May 31, 1942.

Elders' Meeting Minutes. 1895-1920, 1947, 1948.

Ellis, Gilbert J. and J. H. Fillmore, Ed's. *The Praise Hymnal*. Cincinnati, Ohio: Fillmore Brothers, 1896.

Fillmore, James H. *New Christian Hymn and Tune Book*. Cincinnati, Ohio: The Standard Publishing Company, 1882.

Finance Committee Minutes. October 23, 1910; February 2, 1914; and March 2, 1914.

Hymns of Worship and Service. New York: The Century Co., 1911.

Kitzinger, Mrs. Chester. Employment Agreement with Tabernacle Church of Christ.

Miller, Hugh Th. *Tabernacle Church of Christ. Columbus, Indiana History: 1829-1940*. 1940.

Miller, J. Irwin. Letter to Howard Irwin. August 22, 1947.

McKinley, Daniel. Letter to E. Wayne Berry. May 20, 1980.

Poulton, Dorothy F., ed. *Songs for Preschool Children*. Cincinnati, Ohio: The Standard Publishing Company, 1946.

Robinson, T. Earl. Personal Notes on the ministry of T. K. Smith.

Small, James. "The Old Days, The Old Ways and the Old Friends." Columbus, Indiana: The Bartholomew County Christian Missionary Association, 1928.

Trustees of First Christian Church. Letter to Board of Elders and Deacons. November 3, 1948, p. 1.

Private Files

Berry, E. Wayne. Assorted concert programs and newspaper clippings.

Cartwright, Byron James. Assorted concert programs, notes, conversations.

Denny, Mazie. Concert programs.

Dismore, Margaret. Concert and recital programs.

Dismore, Margaret. Interview notes with Josephine Hutchins Schumacher, April 26, 1982.

Tangeman, Clementine Miller. Quilt presented to Z. T. Sweeney by the Ladies Aid Society, 1889.

Online Sources

Many footnotes reference *The Evening Republican*, which evolved into *The Republican*, and then *The Republic*. Former microfilm resources are now available online.

Academia.edu

Amortization.org.

Bach Cantatas website

Bartholomew County Historical Society

Butler Digital Commons

Columbus.in.gov

The Columbus Symphony

Digital Commons @ Columbia College Chicago

Facebook

findagrave.com

Four Freshmen and Five Trombones

Fourfreshmen.com.

Google

History of the Restoration Movement

The Inn at Irwin Gardens

David Secrest. Historiccolumbus.org/jscrump.html.

Indianahistory.org.

Jacobs School of Music, musicindiana.edu.

The Juilliard School

Library of Congress

newspapers.com.

Nytimes.com.

Oneplace.com

Pipeorgandatabase.org.

www.thejoyofmusic.org.

52 Weeks of Columbus, Indiana

About the Author

Music, history, faith, and family have always been interwoven in the life of Byron James Cartwright. After completing a fifty-plus year professional career in music and ministry with two colleges and five congregations, Dr. Cartwright has found time to write during retirement: first, his memoirs, *Connections and Reflections*; second, his introduction to philosophy of music, *All About Music ... Nothing About Music*, and now *Amazing Sounds in a Midwestern Town: Columbus, Indiana: Small City with a Big Musical Heritage*. Dr. Cartwright holds degrees from the Cincinnati Bible Seminary, University of Cincinnati College-Conservatory of Music, and Southern Baptist Theological Seminary in Louisville, Kentucky. He and his wife/soulmate/musician-mate Katie live in Lanett, Alabama. They are the parents of a son and daughter and have five grandchildren.

www.ingramcontent.com/pod-product-compliance
Lightning Source LLC
Chambersburg PA
CBHW031523120626
46545CB00005B/1969